A History of the
People of Israel
c. 1800 B.C.—A.D. 1980

ALICE PARMELEE

Come then, praise the God of the universe, . . .
May he grant us a joyful heart,
and in our time send Israel lasting peace.

Ecclesiasticus 50.22-23, New English Bible

MOREHOUSE-BARLOW CO.
Wilton, Connecticut

The cover illustration is from a tapestry entitled *The Madness of Saul*, which depicts the old king banishing the young David from the palace. From St. Mary's Chapel in the Cathedral Church of Saints Peter and Paul, Washington, D.C. Used by permission.

The Scripture quotations in this book, unless attributed otherwise, are from the Revised Standard Version of the Bible, copyrighted 1946, 1952 ©1971, 1973 by the Division of Christian Education of the National Council of the Churches of Christ in the U.S.A., and used by permission.

Morehouse-Barlow Co., Inc.
78 Danbury Road, Wilton, Connecticut 06897

ISBN 0-8192-1273-3

Library of Congress Catalog Card Number 80-81097

Printed in the United States of America

Contents

Preface

The dramatic and often tragic story of the people of Israel during more than three and a half milleniums is about a community bound together by its belief that, in a unique way, it is the people of God. This book surveys and interprets Israel's story, with special attention to the Biblical period.

Beginning with Abraham, the father of the faithful, Israel's long succession of larger-than-life individuals is reviewed against the historical background and main events of Old Testament times and also of the two centuries preceding the rise of Christianity. In the many transformations of Israel's history, as sketched in the first six parts of this book, we meet: patriarchs, priests, prophets, warriors, tribal chiefs, kings, queens, governors, revolutionaries. Despite their formidable and often difficult-to-pronounce names, and the almost inconceivable situations they faced, these people emerge from the remote past as human beings basically like ourselves.

To complete the story, the last two sections of this book trace Israel's survival and the vicissitudes of the land of Palestine from Roman times to the establishment of the modern state of Israel.

Because the aim of this volume is to shed light on the Scriptures, many Biblical references are given, with the hope that these may induce readers to go to the original documents themselves and fill out this necessarily concise account. Chronology being the backbone of historical understanding, many dates are cited, not because they are hard and fast—most dates of the B.C. era are open to question—but because they help to establish the relationship of events.

The story of the people of Israel is important to us, partly because Abraham's descendants live in our midst today, bearers of the oldest surviving civilization of the western world. Many aspects of their ancient story forcibly remind us of ourselves and our own predicaments. Moreover, the Biblical history is, in a sense, our history, because Israel's faith in one living God who enters into our human life is our faith also—a faith that gives meaning to the unknown, lightens our darkness, heals the unhappiness and suffering of existence, and sets us on the road of life rejoicing.

Many people have contributed to the making of this book and to all of them I am grateful: to the 20th-century English translators of the Old Testament and the Apocrypha, who have made the Scriptural sources easily available; to the historians, archaeologists, and other scholars, whose works explain much that was previously obscure in Hebrew history and make possible a comprehensive view, like this one; to all those at Morehouse-Barlow Company, whose decisions and actions transformed a stack of typescript into a book; to the Rev. Dr. J. Raymond Lord, who read the manuscript and made useful suggestions; and finally, to my sister, who made the entire undertaking possible.

Alice Parmelee

ABBREVIATIONS

For the Books of the Bible

Old Testament

Genesis	Gen	Ecclesiastes	Eccles
Exodus	Ex	Song of Solomon	Song
Leviticus	Lev	Isaiah	Isa
Numbers	Num	Jeremiah	Jer
Deuteronomy	Deut	Lamentations	Lam
Joshua	Josh	Ezekiel	Ezek
Judges	Judg	Daniel	Dan
Ruth	Ruth	Hosea	Hos
1 Samuel	1 Sam	Joel	Joel
2 Samuel	2 Sam	Amos	Amos
1 Kings	1 Kings	Obadiah	Obad
2 Kings	2 Kings	Jonah	Jonah
1 Chronicles	1 Chron	Micah	Mic
2 Chronicles	2 Chron	Nahum	Nahum
Ezra	Ezra	Habakkuk	Hab
Nehemiah	Neh	Zephaniah	Zeph
Esther	Esther	Haggai	Hag
Job	Job	Zechariah	Zech
Psalms	Ps	Malachi	Mal
Proverbs	Prov		

New Testament

Matthew	Mt	1 Timothy	1 Tim
Mark	Mk	2 Timothy	2 Tim
Luke	Lk	Titus	Titus
John	Jn	Philemon	Philem
Acts of the Apostles	Acts	Hebrews	Heb
Romans	Rom	James	Jas
1 Corinthians	1 Cor	1 Peter	1 Pet
2 Corinthians	2 Cor	2 Peter	2 Pet
Galatians	Gal	1 John	1 Jn
Ephesians	Eph	2 John	2 Jn
Philippians	Phil	3 John	3 Jn
Colossians	Col	Jude	Jude
1 Thessalonians	1 Thess	Revelation	Rev
2 Thessalonians	2 Thess		

Other Abbreviations

A.D.	*Anno Domini*—"in the year of our Lord"
B.C.	Before Christ
c.	*circa*—"about," used with uncertain dates
KJV	King James Version (Authorized Version)
NEB	New English Bible
N.T.	New Testament
O.T.	Old Testament
RSV	Revised Standard Version
v., vv.	Verse, verses

How to Look up Bible References

Jn 3:16—means the Gospel according to John, chapter 3, verse 16

Mic 6:5,8—means the Book of Micah, chapter 6, verse 5 and verse 8

2 Cor 5:17-19—means the Second Letter to the Corinthians, chapter 5, verse 17 to 19 inclusive

Jer 8:7; 9:3—means Jeremiah, chapter 8, verse 7; and also chapter 9, verse 3

Mt 5:2-7:28—means the Gospel according to Matthew, chapter 5, verse 2, to chapter 7, verse 28 inclusive

Mt 5-7—means Matthew, chapter 5 through chapter 7

Mk 8:29; Lk 9:20—means Mark, chapter 8, verse 29; and Luke, chapter 9, verse 20

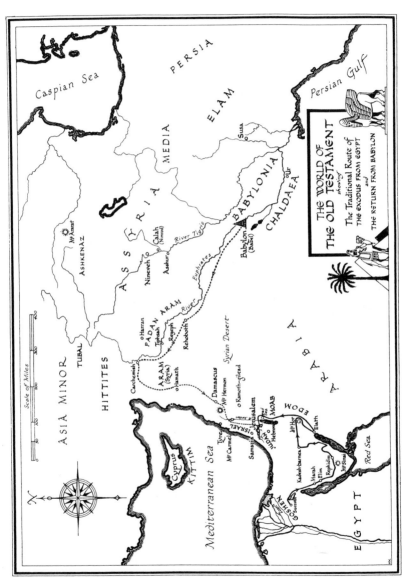

THE WORLD OF
THE OLD TESTAMENT
showing
The Traditional Route of
THE EXODUS FROM EGYPT
and
THE RETURN FROM BABYLON

British & Foreign Bible Society, London

Horace Knowles

Part One

The Emergence of Israel

Chapter 1 **The Age of Abraham**
c. 1800-1700 B.C.

Genesis 11.26-35.29

Israel traced its origin to Abraham, the man of faith divinely chosen to be the father of a special people. His story in Genesis is, in part, the legendary account of a tribal patriarch who lived in the Middle Bronze Age, the period that produced the Babylonian king Hammurabi and the civilization documented on tablets excavated from the Amorite state of Mari. Abraham's story cannot be dismissed as merely the tale of a mythological hero, for much of it agrees with what we now know of the historical background of the period. In the estimation of the archaeologist C. Leonard Woolley, it contains "a considerable stratum of literal truth."

Genesis presents Abraham as a heroic leader, but also as a person who once actually lived and possessed many of the characteristics of our common humanity. Centuries after his era, when Israel's scribes and chroniclers prepared the Biblical account of him, rewriting and revising the traditions in the light of their faith, they found that Abraham's story foreshadowed Israel's history. From his story they learned that God had a purpose for Israel, a divinely appointed mission for his people that no one could thwart. They also saw the reality of God's guidance of his chosen people. Moreover, in Abraham's life lived in the presence of God, and in his faith and obedience, they became aware of the qualities expected of those who belonged to Israel.

Abraham was a semi-nomadic herdsman who came probably from the Aramean branch of the Semitic people. One Biblical tradition indicates that the great imperial city of Ur on the lower reaches of the Euphrates River was his ancestral city. Another tradition places his home in northwestern Mesopotamia at the Amorite city of Haran.

In Abraham's time the ancient Sumerian metropolis of Ur had achieved a high level of civilization, with irrigation, trading, laws, writing, and the beginnings of art and monumental architecture. Modern excavations at this site have revealed the great rampart and wall of the city, its palaces, temples to the moon god, and lofty temple tower, or ziggurat, which may have inspired the story of the tower of Babel. Did Abraham walk through the maze of Ur's winding streets or live in one of its burnt brick houses? Today, guides at the excavations point to a ruined structure and declare, with more imagination than reliable fact, "This was Abraham's house!" Such dwellings often had a second story from which projected a balcony that overlooked the inner courtyard. In this, animals were probably kept and merchandise stored. In the great royal cemetery, by Abraham's day, the early Sumerian kings of Ur had been lying undisturbed for centuries, with all their fabulous golden treasures.

Are Abraham's business records inscribed in cuneiform on some of the thousands of clay tablets recently unearthed from the archives of Ur? If so, his records have not been discovered, for, as Max Mallowan, one of the archaeologists at Ur, writes, "Of Abraham himself . . . we found not a trace." Nevertheless, cuneiform documents not only from Ur but also from Nuzi and Mari in modern Iraq, and the recently discovered palace archives of Ebla in northwest Syria, reveal the social customs, laws, and ways of life familiar to Abraham and the other patriarchs, and, because of their stories, familiar also to Bible readers. Clearly the world of Mesopotamia and beyond, about 1800 B.C., was Abraham's world.

Despite his possible contacts with such great commercial centers as Ur and Haran, Abraham was not primarily a city man. His other world was the desert and the treeless plains of the Fertile Crescent from which his ancestors had come. Because he owned large flocks of sheep and goats, he often moved with the seasons from place to place in search of green pastures. On these journeys he traveled under the vast solitudes of sky unaware that sometimes beneath his feet lay immense deposits of oil that would one day provide the energy for a future civilization.

It was on one of his frequent journeys that the first chapter of Hebrew history begins. Abraham, or Abram as the Bible calls him before the covenant, was preparing to set out from his homeland of Haran with his wife Sarah, their household, and all their creatures, when he heard a voice.

> Now the Lord said to Abram, "Go from your country and your kindred and your father's house to the land that I will show you. And I will make of you a great nation, and I will bless you, and make your name great, so that you will be a blessing . . . . and in you all the families of the earth shall be blessed."
>
> Genesis 12.1-3, with footnote

In an act of faith and obedience, Abraham departed from Haran and headed southward through the Fertile Crescent. This arc of productive land borders the desert and stretches from the Persian Gulf northwest through Mesopotamia to the mountains and then south to the Sinai Peninsula. When he arrived in the sparsely settled hill country of Canaan, Abraham chose a route to the cross-roads city of Shechem and encamped there. At this first city of the Promised Land mentioned in the Bible, he built an altar to the Lord, calling on his name and thereby proclaiming the Lord's dominion over the land. It was at Shechem that Abraham first heard the Lord's promise that continues to reverberate nearly four milleniums later, "To your descendants I will give this land" (Gen 12.7).

Abraham did not experience unbroken success or untroubled faith. His life was one of struggle and the Lord's promises often seemed impossible of fulfillment. As the record shows, he and his descendants suffered in the ordinary way from their own human failings, from life's misfortunes, and from hope deferred. Again and again his faith was tested. When he believed that the Lord required him to sacrifice his son Isaac, on whom all his hopes rested, he prepared to obey.

When Sarah died, because Abraham was still "a stranger and a sojourner" in the land the Lord had promised to him, he was obliged to obtain legal right to a burial place for her. He purchased from Ephron the Hittite, for four hundred shekels worth of carefully weighed-out silver, a plot of land at Machpelah, which is east of Hebron. On the land was the cave in which he buried Sarah. Later, Isaac and his half-brother Ishmael buried their father beside Sarah (Gen 25.9). Today above this burial cave rises a great Moslem mosque. Its name, Haram el Khalil, meaning "Enclosure of the Friend," refers to Abraham, who was known as the friend of God (Isa 41.8). Moslems, as well as Jews, honor Abraham as their father, because from his son Ishmael the twelve Ishmaelite tribes were descended (Gen 25.12-18). Other Arab tribes trace their descent from Abraham and his secondary wife Keturah (Gen 25.1-6).

Though the burial cave beneath Haram el Khalil has not been entered since the 12th century A.D., it is believed to contain not only the tombs of Abraham and Sarah, but of their son of the promise, Isaac, with his wife Rebekah; and of their grandson Jacob, with his wife Leah. Jacob's beloved wife Rachel was buried near Bethlehem where she died.

After Abraham, the most outstanding of the patriarchs is his grandson Jacob. His name, meaning "Supplanter," brings to mind the episode in which he cheated his elder brother Esau of the all-important family birthright. In consequence, he had to flee to the patriarchs' ancestral home in Haran. Here most of his sons were born. On returning to the Promised Land, Jacob had a strange encounter with the Lord at the ford of the Jabbok River, after which his name was changed to Israel, probably meaning "God rules." Thereafter, the twelve tribes descended from Jacob's sons were known as the twelve tribes of Israel, and the whole community that sprang from them was called the people of Israel.

The faith bequeathed by the patriarchs to their descendants is embodied in their stories. To each of these ancient fathers was granted a personal experience of God. They knew him as the ever-present One who spoke to them, guided them, and showed them their own possibilities. He alone caused the seemingly impossible to come to pass. The patriarchs were aware that God's choice of them for special favors went hand in hand with their obligation to obey him and do what is right and just (Gen 18.19). They understood that their privileges and blessings were intended to bless others also (Gen 18.18). Later, because the people of Israel learned about their God from the stories of the patriarchs, they identified him as "the God of your fathers, the God of Abraham, the God of Isaac, and the God of Jacob" (Ex 3.15).

The larger-than-life aspect of the patriarchs in Genesis is due, not to unusual intelligence or to superhuman physical strength, which is the distinguishing mark of heroes in well-known mythologies, but to their faith in God and their obedience to his will. This is the key to their greatness. Their descendants honored them, not for the worldly success that some of them achieved, but for the evidence that they were the friends of God. The aura of divine destiny that surrounds them in the Bible also illuminates the long and often tragic course of Israel's history, making it unlike other histories, which, as the English historian Edward Gibbon said, are "little more than the register of the crimes, follies, and misfortunes of mankind." Israel's history contains its share of "crimes, follies, and misfortunes," but it is also the record of a people who, in their best moments, attempted to be worthy of their calling as the people of God.

Chapter 2 Israel in Egypt
c. 1700-1290 B.C.

Genesis 37-50

Joseph's story, one of the most compelling in the Bible, is based, like all the patriarchal stories, on ancient oral traditions compiled and written with many an embellishment. In the Biblical account, Joseph, born to Jacob in his old age, was the patriarch's favorite son above all his brothers. He was only a shepherd lad of seventeen when his father honored him with the gift of a long robe with sleeves—the "coat of many colors," according to some translations. As it was a far more luxurious garment than the short, sleeveless tunics worn by his ten older brothers, they became jealous of him and resented his superior ways. Finally, when an opportunity arose, they sold Joseph as a slave to a passing caravan of traders bound for Egypt.

In Egypt, Joseph, while unjustly languishing in the royal prison, suggested a practical way to prevent the recurrent famines that afflicted the land. The Pharaoh was so pleased with Joseph's plan that he promptly released him from prison and made him chief minister of state in charge of the proposed agricultural reforms.

Meanwhile, in Canaan, when the seasonal rains failed, the pastures dried up and famine threatened the land. Jacob, learning that there was grain in Egypt, sent his ten sons there to buy provisions for themselves and their animals. Egyptian texts of this period show that it was state policy to allow herdsmen from Asia to pass through the line of border fortresses and enter Egypt "as a favor . . . in order to keep their cattle alive."

Joseph, as the Pharaoh's chief minister, welcomed his brothers to Egypt. In making himself known to them he expressed the patriarchal faith in God's overruling providence and his care of his people.

> "I am your brother, Joseph, whom you sold into Egypt. And now do not be distressed, or angry with yourselves, because you sold me here; for God sent me before you to preserve life. . . . to preserve for you a remnant on earth and to keep alive for you many survivors."
>
> Genesis 45.4-5, 7

Subsequently, the Pharaoh invited Joseph's father and his entire family to leave famine-stricken Canaan and to settle in the lush pasture land of the eastern Nile Delta. Here they were near the new capital established by Egypt's Hyksos rulers, who, some scholars believe, were the Pharaohs of Joseph's story (Gen 45.10).

The Hyksos rulers were Canaanite or Amorite invaders from Syria-Palestine. Because they were armed with superior bows and horse-drawn war chariots—the first the Egyptians had seen—the Hyksos were able to defeat the weak Pharaohs of the Middle Kingdom and reign from their capital in the Delta at Avaris-Tanis (Zoan) for about two hundred years. Finally, a native Egyptian dynasty, the eighteenth, expelled the Hyksos and set out to conquer the world.

According to Biblical tradition, "The time that the people of Israel dwelt in Egypt was four hundred and thirty years" (Ex 12.40; *see also* Gen 15.13; Acts 7.6). If the arrival of the Hebrew tribes in Egypt coincided with the period of the Hyksos rulers, beginning about 1720 B.C., then the exodus from Egypt must have taken place about 1290 B.C.

If Abraham's descendants were indeed in Egypt during the period of the eighteenth dynasty, they probably played little part in the expulsion of the Hyksos or in the establishment of the new Egyptian empire. While the Hebrew tribes "multiplied and grew exceedingly strong" (Ex 1.7), Egypt experienced one of the greatest periods of her early history. Thutmose III, the "Napoleon of ancient Egypt," won a decisive victory in 1469 B.C. over a league of Canaanite kings near Megiddo. This gave him control over Syria and Canaan, which for three centuries comprised a province of Egypt.

Not only from Canaan, but from other conquered parts of the empire, which eventually extended from Nubia at the Fourth Cataract of the Nile north to the Euphrates in Asia, fabulous wealth poured into Egypt. Though it was probably of little benefit to the hard-pressed Hebrew shepherds and farmers, it greatly enriched Egypt. It may have paid for the magnificent temple of Karnak at Thebes and the huge, red granite obelisks set up to glorify Thutmose III. Two of these were originally erected in the lower Nile valley at On (Heliopolis), which was the center of Egyptian sun worship, and the place where the father of Joseph's Egyptian wife, Asenath, was a priest (Gen 41.45). One of these monolithic stone shafts now stands on the Thames Embankment, London, and the other in Central Park, New York City.

Eventually, the rulers of the rich and powerful kingdoms in Canaan and Syria revolted against their overlords and, during the reigns of such Pharaohs as Akhnaton and his young son-in-law Tutankhamun, the vast Egyptian empire began to crumble. Akhnaton adopted the sole worship of the sun god Aton and moved his capital from Thebes down the Nile to the location of Tell el-Amarna. Here were found the so-called Amarna Letters written to the Pharaoh from such places as Ugarit, Gebal, Tyre, Sidon, Damascus, Megiddo, Jerusalem, Shechem. The contents of these letters show that Egyptian power was breaking down in Canaan and beyond.

Egyptian civilization had reached a high point at this time. Akhnaton's great Hymn to the Sun may have become the model for Psalm 104, which was written centuries later. The treasures brought to light in A.D. 1922, after the discovery of Tutankhamun's tomb, illustrate the wealth and cultural achievements of Egypt during the eighteenth dynasty while the Hebrews were living their unrecorded lives in the land of the Nile.

With the rise of the aggressive nineteenth dynasty (c. 1319-1200 B.C.), "there arose a new king over Egypt, who did not know Joseph" (Ex 1.8). The Pharaohs of this new dynasty set out to reconquer the empire in Asia lost by Akhnaton. They moved their capital down the Nile from Thebes to the Delta, where, near the site of the old Hyksos capital, Rameses II built Raamses, or Rameses. Nearby, in the same fortified border area, he built Pithom. On both these building projects the Hebrews worked as forced labor under the lash of taskmasters. But worse was to follow.

The Pharaoh, fearing the presence of aliens on his exposed northeastern frontier, according to the Biblical narrative, exclaimed, "Behold, the people of Israel are too many and too mighty for us. Come, let us deal shrewdly with them . . ." (Ex 1.9-10). He then decreed the death of every male child born to the Hebrews. The promise made to Abraham now seemed doomed to failure. Yet out of this desperate situation would emerge the events from which the community of Israel arose.

Chapter 3 Moses, the Exodus, and the Covenant

c. 1290-1250 B.C.

Exodus 1-24, 32-34

At the critical moment when the descendants of Abraham faced almost certain annihilation in Egypt, there arose among them a truly great and outstanding leader. Moses, according to the scholar and archaeologist, William F. Albright, is "the first great individual in history whose life and personality we can sketch with any degree of clarity." As leader and liberator, lawgiver and judge, prophet and poet, miracle-worker and mediator between God and man, Moses endowed his people with much of the character that made them outstanding among the nations of antiquity. Born to Hebrew parents of the tribe of Levi; saved in infancy by the ingenuity and courage of his mother and sister; given an Egyptian name which means "is born" and which was often part of names like Thutmose; educated, in consequence of an unusual circumstance, at the Egyptian court; awakened to the plight of his people; dangerously implicated in their defense; forced to flee for his life to Midian—so runs his familiar story.

In the desert, at a bush that burned yet was not consumed, the Lord made his presence known to Moses and spoke to him as, long before, he had spoken to Abraham,

> "I am the God of your father, the God of Abraham, the God of Isaac, and the God of Jacob . . . . I have seen the affliction of my people who are in Egypt . . . and I

have come down to deliver them . . . . Come, I will
send you to Pharaoh that you may bring forth my
people, the sons of Israel, out of Egypt."

Exodus 3.6-8, 10

Divinely called to lead his people in this crisis, Moses
became acutely aware of his own human limitations and
shrank from his awesome responsibility. Nevertheless,
fortified as other prophets after him would be by his
certainty in the Lord's purpose and promise, he returned to
Egypt. There, with the help of his brother Aaron, he
appeared before the Pharaoh and appealed to him to free
the people of Israel. The stubborn monarch refused to let
his slaves leave Egypt. Ten devastating plagues against
Egypt finally convinced him that the God of the Israelites
was angry with him. Then, fearful of further calamities, he
abruptly ordered the people of Israel, "Take your flocks
and your herds, as you have said, and be gone" (Ex 12.32).

Free at last, they celebrated their first Passover in haste,
with sandals on their feet and a staff in hand, ready for the
long trek from the land of their oppression. By the time
they reached the Egyptian frontier, however, the Pharaoh's
fear of them had vanished, and, changing his mind, he
ordered his chariots and the well-armed horsemen of his
border patrol to pursue the fugitives.

Ahead of the Israelites stretched an impassable body of
water; behind them the Egyptian chariots and horsemen
drew nearer. They were trapped. There was no time to lose
if they were to be saved from death at the hands of the
Egyptians.

Then Moses stretched out his hand over the sea; and
the Lord drove the sea back by a strong east wind all
night, and made the sea dry land, and the waters were
divided.

Exodus 14.21

The Finding of Moses—Biblia Strasburger, Zurich (1620)

With fidelity to the story in Exodus 2.1-11, the engraver who illustrated this German version of the Bible, portrayed the infant Moses in the midst of a 17th century scene in northern Europe.

With this escape route miraculously opened before them, the people hurriedly gathered together their possessions and, driving their flocks and herds ahead of them, marched across the exposed sea bottom to the opposite shore. The Egyptians followed relentlessly, but the wheels of their chariots stuck in the moist sand. When the waters flowed back, the pursuing force was drowned.

Safe on the far shore, the band of refugees perceived their deliverance as an act of God that revealed his presence with them. The miracle at the sea was to them the Lord's victory and in their exaltation they knew that they were indeed a people over whom the Lord was extending his protecting hand to liberate and to redeem. In the hour of this holy event their faith was born, and, in words attributed to Moses' sister Miriam, they sang their first hymn of praise:

> Sing to the Lord, for he has triumphed gloriously;
> the horse and his rider he has thrown into the sea.
>
> Exodus 15.21

The song, one of the most ancient in the Bible, is a prelude to Israel's long tradition of "the poetry of faith." The historical event itself was a notable part of the recitation of the mighty acts of God, which became their creed.

Other dangers and difficulties now faced the people of Israel. A series of heavily guarded Egyptian fortresses protected the main military and commercial highway leading northward, so that Moses dared not lead his people directly into Canaan by this well-traveled coastal road. He therefore turned southward with his crowd of untrained and undisciplined ex-slaves and led them through the thinly settled desolation of the Sinai Peninsula. Here, when they encountered hunger and thirst, they complained bitterly, but the Lord manifested his care and protected his people. Always they could see him going before them in what they perceived as a pillar of cloud by day and a pillar of fire by night.

At length they came to the awesome granite mountain called Sinai, or in some records Horeb, and pitched their camp in its shadow. Here occurred the most important event of their years in the wilderness and also the most significant event of their entire history. At this mountain, amid thunder and lightning, they "heard the voice of the living God speaking out of the midst of the fire" (Deut 5.26). Their God, whom they called Yahweh, established his covenant with the people of Israel, binding them to himself in a permanent union (Ex 19.4-6). For their part, the people ratified the covenant "with one voice." This covenant became the central reality of Israel's life, and they regarded themselves as the people of the covenant. In this act of dedication, they acknowledged that, by his "mighty hand" and his "many signs and wonders," God had delivered them from Egypt and preserved them as his people—a people with a divine mission. They therefore, in gratitude and obedience, pledged themselves to his service.

Henceforth, they placed themselves under the authority of Yahweh. Out of their common worship of one Lord, the God of Abraham, Isaac, and Jacob, the tribes, together with the "mixed multitude" that had accompanied them from Egypt, began to forge a sense of common purpose and community and to become one people.

At this time Moses brought to them the statutes of the Ten Commandments, which, in a brief form, taught them the character of their Lord and his basic requirements. The ritual duties of the Ten Commandments are few, but a person's right relations with God and with other people are given in greater detail. These include truth, purity, uprightness, goodness, and justice.

When Moses presided as judge over the disputes of his

people, he applied the Lord's standards of righteousness to the day-to-day life of individuals. He also became Israel's first prophet, interpreting the events of past, present, and future in the light of Israel's God.

The Ark of the Covenant, a chest of acacia wood overlaid with gold, was fashioned during Israel's years in the wilderness, and in it were kept the stone tablets "written with the finger of God." Israel believed that Yahweh was invisibly enthroned upon this portable Ark. Because the Ark was not itself an image, the people were not tempted to worship it, as many of their neighbors worshiped the images of their gods. The Ark remained a symbol of Yahweh's abiding presence with his people and for many years it served as the focus of their worship of him. Wherever they journeyed they carried it with them as a moveable sign that the place to which they had come was Yahweh's territory and that he was still with them.

Chapter 4 **The Conquest and Settlement of Canaan**

c. 1250-1050 B.C.

Numbers 11-14; 21-24; Joshua 1-12; 24;
Judges 2-16; 1 Samuel 4

After many years of hardship and strife in the wilderness, spent mostly at the oasis of Kadesh-barnea south of the Negeb, Moses led his people toward Canaan. When he found that enemies controlled the direct route northward, he proceeded toward the east, skirting unfriendly Edom and Moab and finally reaching the Transjordan. Here the Israelites encamped on the Plains of Moab opposite Jericho.

From their encampment, Moses climbed Mount Nebo, also named Pisgah, surveying the whole panorama of the Promised Land from Dan and the Sea of Galilee in the far north to Beersheba and the Negeb in the south, and from the Western Sea to the Jordan Valley with "Jericho the city of palm trees." He was destined to see but not to enter the land to which he had led his people, for somewhere on the mountain he died, "but no man knows the place of his burial to this day" (Deut 32.48-52; 34).

In Joshua, whom Moses had chosen and trained to be his successor, the Israelites gained a courageous military leader who was loyal to Israel's cause and able to inspire his men to fight for the "land flowing with milk and honey" that lay before them.

With an auspicious crossing of the Jordan River, Joshua's campaign began. At the harvest season, the Jordan usually overflows its banks, but, when Joshua led Israel across the

river, its bed was dry, probably because a landslide up-
stream had blocked the water's flow. To the people this
was a sign that once more the Lord was with them as he
had been on their departure from Egypt.

The Book of Joshua seems to describe a single brilliant
campaign during which Joshua subdued the entire land of
Canaan. When the Books of Joshua and Judges are carefully
read, however, they confirm what archaeological research
has revealed—that Israel's conquest of the Promised Land
was neither sudden nor complete. At this time Egypt had
lost her hold over Canaan, and the warring city-states and
petty kingdoms of the region were unable to act together.
Moreover, Assyria had not yet begun what was to become
its inexorable westward expansion. Nevertheless, despite
the absence of any powerfully organized opposition, the
invading Hebrew tribes encountered Canaanites armed
with weapons far more effective than their own and a
people with a higher level of civilization than that of Israel.
The Hebrew conquest and settlement of Canaan, therefore,
was a long and complicated process.

Joshua and his men often captured and destroyed cities
like Jericho, Bethel, and Hazor. At other times the Hebrew
tribes gradually filtered into the land and merged with the
native Canaanites or with related tribes already living in
Canaan. In this way, cities like Gibeon and Shechem were
peacefully absorbed into Israel's realm. Some strongly
fortified cities like Jerusalem were simply by-passed by the
invaders. Jerusalem was left in the control of the Jebusites
until the reign of David two centuries after the conquest.

Upon reaching Canaan the tribes of Israel organized
themselves and related tribes into a loose confederacy and
renewed their covenant with the Lord at their chief
sanctuary in the ancient Canaanite city of Shechem. Later
the sanctuary was moved to Shiloh in the central mountain
range. Such unity as their tribal confederacy possessed

arose from their common faith in Yahweh and from the remembrance of the exodus from Egypt and their conquest of the Promised Land. They made solemn pledges of peace and mutual defence, but, despite these unifying forces, tribal feuds often broke out. The distinctiveness of Israel as the people of Yahweh was further endangered by their intermarriage with the Canaanites and their wide-spread adoption of local Baal-worship.

To each tribe was assigned its own portion of the land. The process of changing from a nomadic, tribal existence to a settled, agricultural life proved to be long and difficult. The settlers dug wells and cisterns, established farms on land reclaimed from deserts and forests, and built small, unfortified towns quite different in character and purpose from the former Canaanite strongholds they had subdued.

During this period of struggle and settlement, the tribes were ruled by leaders called "judges." When some danger threatened Israel's precarious foothold in Canaan or when raiding parties of Moabites, Midianites, or Ammonites plundered them, groups of beleaguered tribes often united temporarily under one of the judges to repel the enemy.

Deborah the prophetess was one of these judges. She roused five of the scattered tribes to the danger posed by a group of Canaanite states that had not only allied themselves against Israel but had raised a formidable army equipped with iron chariots and commanded by Sisera. Undaunted by the force arrayed against her people, Deborah summoned Barak, the Israelite general, to lead the poorly armed Israelite forces and said to him, "The Lord, the God of Israel, commands you, 'Go, gather your men at Mount Tabor. . . . and I will give him [Sisera] into your hand'" (Judg 4.6-7). Faith such as this at times transformed the scattered and ill-prepared Israelites into a determined force able, as they were in the great battle at Megiddo, of defending their territory from hostile attacks.

Another instance of the tribes joining forces in a crisis occurred when the judge Gideon, a hero of the tribe of Manasseh, assembled a volunteer group from the northern tribes and decisively repelled a band of nomadic Midianite raiders. Partly out of gratitude to Gideon for this triumph, but also to voice their need for a strong central government capable of dealing with further emergencies, the Israelites tried to make Gideon their king. "Rule over us," they begged, "you and your son and your grandson also" (Judg 8.22). But Gideon, convinced that Israel's only king was Yahweh and that obedience to him was the source of the strength and unity of the tribes, refused the hereditary kingship, saying, "I will not rule over you, and my son will not rule over you; the Lord will rule over you" (Judg 8.23).

In defending themselves from the depredations of nomadic raiders, the Israelites also gave protection to the Canaanites among whom they lived. In this way the two groups drew closer together and the Israelites gained more control of Canaan by protecting the native inhabitants than by conquering and destroying them.

By the end of the 12th century Israel faced a far more serious threat to her existence than any previously made by neighboring peoples or marauding nomads from the east. In the west, along the southern coastal plain appeared a highly organized, aggressive people, the Philistines. They were Indo-Europeans belonging to the Sea Peoples who, having been uprooted from Asia Minor and the Aegean Islands, disturbed the political balance of the Middle East in their search for new homes. Some of the Philistines settled in Crete. Others, about 1180 B.C., after being driven from Egypt by Rameses III, settled along Canaan's coast, seizing Gaza, which was Egypt's administrative capital of Canaan, and thus ending the Egyptian domination of the land. The Philistines built five city-states on the coastal plain and united themselves in a strong well-organized federation. Their country became known as Philistia, a name later applied to the entire region in the form "Palestine."

The tales of Samson, the folk hero and judge, indicate the growing peril to Israel's survival from this formidable adversary on her western border. With their advanced civilization and their ability to make weapons of iron—a much harder metal than the bronze used by the Israelites— the Philistines were militarily far superior to the tribes in the central highlands. Their raiding parties could plunder the countryside of Ephraim and Judah at will. Finally, about 1050 B.C., the Philistines set out to win supremacy over Israel.

From the beginning, when the Israelites suffered defeat at the hands of the Philistines in a pitched battle near Aphek, they realized that their existence as the united people of the Lord was at stake. In their extremity, they sent to the sanctuary at Shiloh for the Ark of the Covenant, hoping that this sacred chest would, like a talisman, protect them. The Philistines, however, slaughtered them, captured the Ark of the Lord, razed Shiloh, and became masters of all the land west of the Jordan. The national unity of Israel was now in jeopardy, with its central sanctuary obliterated; its old priest and judge, Eli, and his sons dead; and the Ark, the symbol of God's presence among his people, in enemy hands. Once again, the very survival of the people of God was at stake.

Chapter 5 **Samuel Preserves Israel**

c. 1050-1020 B.C.

1 Samuel 1-12, 15

The man of the desperate hour when the Philistines overran Israel and threatened to destroy her was Samuel—priest, prophet, judge, and kingmaker. The story of his early life is really that of his mother, Hannah, one of Israel's most revered women. Her song of thanksgiving became, ten centuries later, the model for Mary's Magnificat (1 Sam 2.1-10; cf. Lk 1.46-55). Scholars believe that the record of Samuel's life in the First Book of Samuel contains two interwoven and sometimes conflicting accounts: the Early Source, written in the 10th century B.C., and the Late Source, written about two centuries later but based on much earlier records.

In Samuel's boyhood, according to the Late Source, while he ministered to the Lord in the national sanctuary at Shiloh under Eli's direction, one of his duties was to tend the lamp that burned continually before the veil of testimony, which hid the Ark from view (1 Sam 3.3; Lev 24.2). One night, while guarding this lamp, Samuel received a prophetic call from God, and a clear word of judgment against Eli and his sons.

During this period, the spiritual foundation of Israel's strength and unity was endangered by the crude nature gods of Canaan—Baal and his consort Ashtoreth, or Asherah. Many of the Lord's people who worshiped Yahweh as the Father of Israel, the God of the covenant, and the Lord not only of nature but of all history as well, had succumbed to Canaanite nature worship. Its fertility rites were practiced in order to propitiate and control Baal and Ashtoreth and thus increase the fruitfulness of the land. This farmer's religion was incompatible with faith in the Lord God who said, "You shall have no other gods before me" (Ex 20.3).

Moreover, Israel's own religion was further debased by corruption in the priesthood, notably that of Eli's unworthy sons, Hophni and Phinehas. In contrast to their evil ways was young Samuel's selfless devotion to Israel and his openness to the word of the Lord. Soon he "was established as a prophet of the Lord" (1 Sam 3.20), one to whom the Lord revealed his will. Thus Samuel was ready, when the Philistines overwhelmed the land, to guide Israel through a precarious time of spiritual and political uncertainty.

With the Ark in enemy hands, the Shiloh sanctuary in ruins, and the old priest Eli dead from the shock of the calamity, Samuel apparently returned to his home in Ramah in the hill country of Benjamin. He was then only a young man, probably about twenty. Despite the disorders of the time, he began to serve the people as one who spoke wisely and truly for the Lord. He had to travel from place to place, for there was no longer one religious center acknowledged by all the tribes. Every year he made a circuit through the central highlands, going from Ramah, to Gilgal, to Mizpah, and finally to Bethel. Although he did not belong to the priestly family, he undertook the priestly duties of building altars and offering sacrifices. He also judged disputes in accordance with the ethical standards of Israel's religion. Wherever he went, his words and actions touched the deepest needs of a people suffering under foreign domination. Gradually, while he restored the people's confidence in themselves and their faith in their Lord, he became "a man that is held in honor" (1 Sam 9.6) and the person to whom everyone turned to learn the will of the Lord.

One day, while Samuel was acting as judge of the harassed tribes that had gathered at Mizpah, the Philistines attacked them. Throughout the ensuing battle Samuel prayed to the Lord while the Israelites succeeded in temporarily routing their attackers. This unexpected victory awoke hope that Israel would soon throw off the Philistine yoke. To commemorate the triumph, Samuel set up a stone named Ebenezer, meaning, "to this point the Lord has helped us" (1 Sam 7.12, NEB).

For many years, Samuel walked before the people as their leader in the presence of God, until, according to the ancient word-picture, he became "old and grey" and, in his comings and goings, he was known as the "old man . . . wrapped in a robe" (1 Sam 12.2; 28.14). Finally, he knew that there was one more service he must perform for the people—he must institute a new and more effective way of governing Israel. The old tribal confederacy depended on some inspired leader, like Deborah or Gideon, to unite the scattered tribes and lead them to victory. This confederacy, however, was no longer politically effective against a determined aggressor. If Philistine domination were to be broken, the people must band together under a strong and permanent ruler. Israel must have a king. The Early Source of Samuel differs from the Late Source in its traditions both of Samuel and of the formation of the monarchy. In the Early Source (1 Sam 9.1-10.16; 11), Samuel is depicted as a priest and prophet who, in obedience to God's will, chooses Saul as king. On the other hand, in the Late Source (1 Sam 7.3-8.22; 10.17-27; 12) Samuel appears as Israel's last and greatest judge who initially objected to the kingship as incompatible with the Kingship of Yahweh. This second view may not only preserve an old tradition but also, especially in 1 Samuel 8.10-18, reflect the people's bitter experiences with their later kings.

The story from the Early Source describes how Samuel met and secretly anointed Saul of the tribe of Benjamin as the Lord's choice for Israel's first king. The old priest's words, as he poured oil from a vial on the head of the tall young man, set Saul apart for the kingship and also clearly established the purpose and constitution of the new monarchy. Its purpose was to protect Israel. The community itself was to remain a theocratic state ruled by God, its true King.

> "Has not the Lord anointed you to be prince over his people Israel? And you shall reign over the people of the Lord and you will save them from the hand of their enemies round about." 1 Samuel 10.1

At the end of the anointing ceremony, the prophet directed the young king to wait seven days "until I come to you and show you what you shall do" (1 Sam 10.8). From these words, Saul learned that the Lord would continue to direct the affairs of Israel through his spokesman, Samuel. It would be the young king's duty to obey the divine guidance received by the old prophet from the Lord.

As Samuel's subsequent troubled relations with him reveal, Saul did not live up to the prophet's fundamental requirement. Instead of carrying out the Lord's will, Saul followed his own. Because of Saul's disobedience, Samuel broke with the king and "did not see Saul again until the day of his death, but Samuel grieved over Saul" (1 Sam 15.35). Nevertheless, Samuel did not replace the king, though there is a well-known story that he secretly anointed David to be Saul's eventual successor (1 Sam 16.1-13).

Because of Samuel's life-long devotion to the welfare of Israel, his uncompromising belief in God as the true ruler of the community, and his prophetic insistence on obedience to the Lord ("to obey is better than sacrifice," 1 Sam 15.22), he not only helped to preserve Israel during a period of change, but he enabled her to achieve a fuller spiritual life.

Part Two
Kings of the United Kingdom

Chapter 6 **Saul Establishes the Monarchy**
c. 1020-1000 B.C.

1 Samuel 9-31; 2 Samuel 1

Saul, son of Kish, a wealthy man of the tribe of Benjamin, first became prominent in Israel when, as a young man he rescued Jabesh-gilead from the Ammonites beyond the Jordan. His commanding presence together with his courage and resourcefulness in battle captured the imagination of the people and convinced them that he could deliver them from their most dangerous foe, the Philistines. According to one report, the prophet Samuel introduced Saul to the tribes assembled at Gilgal, saying, "Do you see him whom the Lord has chosen?" In reply, the people acclaimed the tall young man as their king, shouting with one accord, "Long live the king!" (1 Sam 10.24)

Saul established his capital at Gibeah, which was his home, in the central highlands of Benjamin. Here he built a massive stronghold whose citadel with its masonry walls, ten feet in thickness, today attests to his determination to defend the tribes against the Philistines. From this fortress, Saul and his volunteer followers went out to strike the first effective blows against the enemy.

For Israel it was an unequal struggle because the politically well-organized Philistines controlled all of Palestine from a series of strong garrisons scattered throughout the land. Furthermore, they had learned how to forge iron and fashion such things as swords, spear tips, arrows, agricultural tools, and the iron rims of chariot wheels. The softer bronze weapons of the Israelites proved to be no match for the Philistine arms. The Philistines guarded their monopoly of the manufacture of iron (1 Sam 13.19-22). As a result, though Saul, with the help of his valiant son Jonathan, tried in every way to outwit and outfight the enemy, he was obliged to continue struggling against them throughout his reign.

Other difficulties beset Saul. He was unable to unite under his central authority the diverse and highly individual tribes living in the various areas of the country. After his clash with Samuel over the old priest's authority, he lost the endorsement of Israel's chief religious leader. Because of his suspiciousness, his relations with his popular young armor-bearer, David, changed to outright hostility. Thus, despite his deeply religious nature (1 Sam 14.37), his brilliance as a military leader, and his many successes in battle, Saul is pictured in the Bible as a failure and one of its most tragic figures.

In his final battle against the Philistines, three of Saul's sons were killed on Mount Gilboa, and his army was routed. Badly wounded himself in this last desperate effort to defend his people, the king fell on his own sword. Israel was thus once more forced to bow to Philistine might.

Notwithstanding this defeat, Saul left the community in a stronger position than he had found it. By winning many battles, he had taught Israel to stand up against the Philistines. He had earned the people's confidence and kept their loyalty to the end.

A notable aspect of his reign was the beginning of the iron age in Israel. Not only did he and his son Jonathan obtain for themselves iron swords and spears, which were far more effective than their older bronze weapons (1 Sam

13.22), but also the Israelites apparently learned from the Philistines their closely guarded secret of smelting iron. With this knowledge, David and Solomon were later able to arm their forces with up-to-date weapons. The earliest iron plowshare so far discovered in Palestine was dug out of the ruins of Saul's fortress of Gibeah—a harbinger of agricultural and industrial developments. In succeeding reigns, these created the material prosperity that made Israel a power in the region.

David's stirring praise is the last estimate of Saul in the Bible:

> "Thy glory, O Israel, is slain upon thy high places!
>   How are the mighty fallen!
>
> • • • • • • • • • • • • • •
>
> "Saul and Jonathan, beloved and lovely!
>   In life and in death they were not divided;
> they were swifter than eagles,
>   they were stronger than lions.
>
> • • • • • • • • • • • • • •
>
> "Ye daughters of Israel, weep over Saul,
>   who clothed you daintily in scarlet,
>   who put ornaments of gold upon your apparel.
>
> • • • • • • • • • • • • • •
>
> "How are the mighty fallen,
>   and the weapons of war perished!"
>
>   2 Samuel 1.19, 23-24, 27

Chapter 7 David Transforms Israel into a Major State

c. 1000-961 B.C.

1 Samuel 16-2 Samuel 24; 1 Kings 1.1-2.11

At the time of Saul's tragic death in battle, David, though the king's daughter was his wife, had long been outlawed from the kingdom. He now lived in the southern lowlands at Ziklag where he had become a vassal of the Philistines. Some in Israel, however, still recalled his youth as Jesse's youngest son, guarding his father's sheep on the hills around Bethlehem. His anointing by the old priest Samuel had been a secret event, yet everyone remembered his brilliant exploits for Israel and the loyalty he could inspire as a leader of men.

After mourning for Saul and Jonathan, David moved his household to Hebron in the territory of the tribe of Judah and there he persuaded the elders to anoint him king of Judah. Meanwhile, Abner, the general of Saul's army, having escaped from the slaughter at Mount Gilboa, took Saul's only surviving son, Ishbosheth, across the Jordan to Mahanaim and induced the northern tribes to crown him their king. These developments indicate that, even before a united kingdom was securely established, the shepherds of the southern highlands and the prosperous farmers of the northern tribes were drawing apart. The Philistines saw this fundamental diversity as an effective obstacle to the rise of a strong Hebrew kingdom on their eastern flank. They also underestimated the determination and ability of David, their former vassal. Thus, when he became king of Judah, they made no effort to curb his power.

The records of his reign can be read in what is now identified as the Early Source of the Books of Samuel.

These records, combined with later materials, are found in 1 and 2 Samuel and 1 Kings 1-2. They constitute the earliest-known history book in the world—an achievement that in the Court History of David (2 Sam 9-20; 1 Kings 1-2) is notable for its objectivity and its graphic, convincing style. The search for the author of these invaluable records focuses on some contemporary of David who could write and who participated in certain of the events. One of two prominent priests at David's court have been suggested: Abiathar, a descendant of the old priest Eli and sole survivor of the massacre at Nob; or Ahimaaz, who remained loyal to David during the rebellion of his son Absalom. About six centuries later, this Early Source, and especially its Court History of David, provided the author of Chronicles with materials for reconstructing a long account of David as the ideal king (1 Chron 11-29).

David spent his seven years as king of Judah strengthening his position at Hebron. Meanwhile, in the north, Saul's son Ishbosheth was too weak to unite Israel or lead her against the Philistines. It was not, however, until Ishbosheth accused Abner of treason in aspiring to the kingship that the old warrior with twenty of his men defected to David. Soon the leaders of the northern tribes came to Hebron to anoint David as their king. Now that he reigned over all the Hebrew tribes, he began to transform a once disorganized and subject people into the dominant state of the Middle East.

His first move was to storm the hitherto impregnable hilltop fortress of Jerusalem still held by the Canaanites, here locally called Jebusites. After capturing the stronghold on Mount Zion, which had always threatened the security of Israel and Judah, David established the capital of his united kingdom in this strategic city, which became the personal domain of his long-lasting dynasty. As this old Jebusite center was untouched by Hebrew tribal rivalries,

Metropolitan Museum of Art, gift of J. Pierpont Morgan

David and Goliath—Silver Plate (c. 630)

Largest of the ten David plates found on Cyprus in 1902, this one, which is nearly twenty inches in diameter, includes three scenes from 1 Samuel 17.40-51. Emperor Heraclitus I probably ordered the imperial silversmiths of Constantinople to make this David series in order to commemorate his victory over the Persians in 625. Due to his own single-handed combat with the Persian general Ragatis, this scene doubtless had special meaning for the emperor.

both Israelites and Judeans could meet here as equals and friends. Furthermore, with elaborate ceremonies, he brought into Jerusalem the Ark of the Covenant, Israel's sacred symbol, thus making it Israel's Holy City, the city of the Lord, the city that embodied the spirit of a people.

The Philistines, finally realizing that David's control of Jerusalem threatened their trade routes through the central highlands, attacked him in two battles in the Valley of Rephaim south of the Holy City. David defeated them decisively in both engagements, driving them back to their cities in the coastal plain, depriving them of their status as the dominant power in Palestine, and finally reducing them to a tribute-paying vassal.

After subduing the remaining Canaanite cities scattered within Israel's territory, David brought the whole land under one ruler for the first time in history. He won popular support for his reign by improving the organization of his kingdom, and by maintaining "law and justice among all his people" (2 Sam 8.15, NEB).

His next undertaking was to secure his boundaries against threats of neighbors on his eastern and northern flanks. One after another he attacked and defeated Moab, Edom, and Ammon until the entire region east of the Jordan and the Dead Sea was subject to his control. He then advanced north into Syria, establishing garrisons in Damascus and other Aramaean cities and exacting tribute from Toi, king of the Hittite kingdom of Hamath on the Orontes River. With Hiram, king of Tyre and lord of Phoenicia, David entered into an economic alliance. As a result of these conquests and alliances, he became the most powerful ruler of his day, and immense wealth from tribute and trade poured into Jerusalem. Egypt and Assyria, the great powers of the Middle East, were at this time in temporary eclipse, thus enabling David to bequeath to his son Solomon an empire extending from the great bend of the Euphrates south to the Gulf of Aqaba and thence northwest to the Philistine city of Gaza near the Egyptian border. "For he had dominion over all the region west of the Euphrates from Tiphsah to Gaza, over all the kings west of the Euphrates" (1 Kings 4.24).

The various parts of David's realm were held together by his personal popularity, his successes as a military commander, and his ability as an organizer and ruler of a major state. Old tribal jealousies, however, were not forgotten in the emergence of the vital new nation, as is apparent in the two unsuccessful revolts against him. In the first, his son Absalom enlisted the support of malcontents from every part of Israel and stirred up hostility among those Judeans who were angry with David for moving his capital from Hebron to Jerusalem. In the second revolt, Sheba, of the tribe of Benjamin, raised a war cry among the northern tribes, saying,

> "We have no portion in David,
>> and we have no inheritance in the son of Jesse;
>> every man to his tents, O Israel!"

> 2 Samuel 20.1

David stilled this cry, but the discontent smoldered. Later, when the cry was raised against David's grandson, King Rehoboam, it touched off a revolt of the northern tribes and caused the disruption of the united kingdom of David and Solomon (1 Kings 12.16).

Amid the extraordinary accomplishments of David's reign and the royal splendor of his court, with his many wives and ambitious sons, appear the dark shadows of intrigues, vengeance, treason, adultery, rape, murder, and fratricide. David's story depicts the ruler of a people just emerging from barbarism. It is a portrait drawn from life. Yet the dark events of his crude and cruel age often contrast with the king's own warm-heartedness, his generosity and loyalty, his honorable behavior toward a defeated enemy, and his consideration for the helpless. In these respects he was ahead of his time.

David's greatness of character and his basic devotion to the Lord are clearly evident in the story of his encounter with the prophet Nathan. David had committed a great wrong in seducing Bathsheba, the wife of one of his warriors, Uriah the Hittite. Desiring to marry Bathsheba, the king ordered that Uriah be sent into an exposed position in battle against the Ammonites so that he would be killed. After Uriah's death, Nathan entered the king's presence and told him the story of the poor man's one ewe lamb, which a rich man, too mean to use one of his own flock, seized and served up to a traveler.

Angered by the story of this evil deed, David declared, "The man who has done this deserves to die!" Nathan then revealed the meaning of his parable. Pointing to the king, he boldly uttered the fateful words:

> "You are the man! . . . Why have you despised the word of the Lord, to do what is evil in his sight? You have smitten Uriah the Hittite with the sword, and have taken his wife to be your wife, and have slain him with the sword of the Ammonites."
>
> 2 Samuel 12.7-9

What other absolute monarch of that savage age would have tolerated such a denunciation and the ensuing threat? As a man of faith, David heard in the prophet's words a true message from the Lord and, abasing himself, he cried out, "I have sinned against the Lord."

Such was the king who, in a sense, was the real founder of the Hebrew nation and one of the greatest rulers to sit upon the throne of Israel. He gave Israel a defensible capital of great natural beauty, the City of David. By bringing the Ark of the Covenant into Jerusalem he created a religious center for the tribes. He changed Saul's formless government into a more efficient one. He organized a standing army. He raised the state to its zenith of power, making Israel great among its neighbors.

The optimism, prosperity, and imperial glory of the state during his reign encouraged literary activity. As we have seen, the Early Source of Samuel was probably begun at this time. David himself was credited with a gift for music and poetry and some of the psalms, if not actually composed by him, may have originated at this time.

Through the entire record of David runs the theme of his loyalty and devotion to the Lord and his dream of a better world in which God shall be truly known. In the beautiful prayer of praise and thanksgiving attributed to him, the spirit of David's life finds expression.

> Then King David went into the presence of the Lord and took his place there and said, "What am I, Lord God, and what is my family, that thou hast brought me thus far? . . . Thou hast established thy people Israel as thy own for ever, and thou, O Lord, hast become their God . . . . be pleased now to bless thy servant's house that it may continue always before thee; thou, O Lord God, hast promised, and thy blessing shall rest upon thy servant's house for evermore."
>
> 2 Samuel 7.18-29, NEB

Chapter 8 Solomon Consolidates the Kingdom
c. 961-922 B.C.

1 Kings 1.11-11.43; 1 Chronicles 29;
2 Chronicles 1.1-9.31

Solomon, with the help of his mother, Bathsheba, King David, his dying father, Zadok the priest, and Nathan the prophet, thwarted the intrigue of his older half-brother to seize the throne. At David's command, Zadok, Nathan, and Benaiah, the general commanding the king's foreign bodyguard of "mighty men," accompanied Solomon as he rode upon the king's mule down to Gihon. This is a spring in the Kidron Valley below the walls of Jerusalem. There young Solomon was anointed king of Israel and Judah.

> Zadok the priest took the horn of oil from the Tent of the Lord and anointed Solomon; they sounded the trumpet and all the people shouted, "Long live King Solomon!" Then all the people escorted him home in procession, with great rejoicing and playing of pipes, so that the very earth split with the noise.
>
> 1 Kings 1.39-40, NEB

The record of the forty-year reign that began with these rejoicings is preserved in the First Book of Kings. Only the founding of Solomon's kingship, however, comes from the incomparable Early Source, for this contemporary history is largely of David's reign and ends with 1 Kings 2. Centuries later, the next nine chapters were compiled from various documents now lost, such as the "Acts of Solomon" (1 Kings 11.41). Though these chapters are believed to preserve much reliable material, they present Solomon as an aloof, imperial figure who seems to lack the intensely human qualities of his father as depicted in the Early Source. In 1 and 2 Chronicles, written even later than 1 Kings 2-11, both David and his son appear as ideal, but remote, figures.

Solomon, who was probably only about twenty years old when his father died, began his reign with a noble aim and a sense of his responsibility to God for governing wisely. In a dream, the Lord appeared to him and he prayed,

> ". . . Give thy servant, therefore, a heart with skill to listen, so that he may govern the people justly and distinguish good from evil. For who is equal to the task of governing this great people of thine?"
>
> 1 Kings 3.9, NEB

Besides a wise and understanding heart, the young king also desired fame and the worldly honor that wealth and power bring. In a dream it was revealed to him that God would give him all that he desired. But he did not ask what the Lord would have *him* do, for, unlike the greatest of the Hebrews, he was chiefly concerned with what the Lord would do for him. This is the key to his character and his reign.

Solomon's years in power were largely untroubled by warfare. In contrast to his father, he was no fighter. Yet he became an astute politician, administrator, and business man, transforming the empire he inherited from David into a well-organized, wealthy state. He made treaties, not war, with neighboring states and often secured these treaties by his marriage alliances with princesses from Egypt, Moab,

Edom, Sidon, and the Hittite kingdom. His first marriage alliance was with the Pharaoh's daughter, who brought him as her dowry the stronghold of Gezer, recently captured by the Egyptians from the Canaanites. For this Egyptian wife, he built a palace in Jerusalem near his other palaces and royal buildings north of David's city.

Solomon was the first famous builder among the Hebrews. Because at this time they lacked the necessary skills, the king appealed to his ally and business partner Hiram of Tyre for carpenters, masons, and metal-workers. With their help Solomon erected the first Temple in Jerusalem. Built north of his own palace, it served initially as the royal chapel, but later it became the focus of Israel's worship. It was a long, narrow, beautifully decorated structure, measuring about thirty by ninety feet and forty-five feet in height, and built of cut white limestone and cedar planks imported from the great groves of Lebanon. This Temple, whose innermost shrine, the Holy of Holies, symbolized the profound idea that God dwelt among his people, created an impressive center for Israel's increasingly splendid and elaborate worship.

To defend his empire, Solomon constructed a series of fortifications throughout the realm, especially at such strategic cities as Hazor, Gezer, and Megiddo. As the volunteer forces of the old tribal days were no longer adequate, he raised a large standing army equipped with up-to-date iron weapons, added a powerful cavalry, and introduced a fleet of war chariots.

Fabulous wealth poured into his coffers from many sources. Yearly tribute of grain, cattle, sheep, and "fatted fowl" was brought to him from the vassal states his father had subdued. By his time the camel had been domesticated for transportation through arid regions. Consequently, camel caravans plied the international trade routes through his peaceful kingdom and paid the tolls Solomon levied on their rich merchandise. Huge profits came to him from his copper and iron mines in the valley of the Arabah south of the Dead Sea and those near the port of Ezion-geber. He also carried on a profitable trade in horses from Cilicia, chariots from Egypt, and spices, gold, and precious stones from the Queen of Sheba's kingdom in southern Arabia. He operated jointly with King Hiram of Tyre a flotilla of merchant ships that sometimes returned from their long voyages in the Red Sea and Indian Ocean with such exotic cargoes as gold, silver, ivory, apes, and monkeys or peacocks.

Solomon became an influential ruler in the international world of his day, thus moving isolated and backward Israel into the mainstream of the civilization of the Middle East. Friendly relations with Tyre introduced Israel to Canaan's old and rich culture. At Ras Shamra, the site of the ancient Syrian city of Ugarit, there was unearthed in 1929 an extensive library of cuneiform tablets that help us understand the pervasive influence of Canaanite thought and customs on Hebrew life. Though contact with other peoples and their ideas enriched Israel in many ways, the introduction of strange gods and foreign religious practices eventually weakened her religious unity and provoked opposition to the monarchy on the part of those faithful to Yahweh.

To increase his authority over Israel and also to collect taxes more effectively, Solomon reorganized his kingdom, dividing it into twelve administrative districts each headed by an official responsible to him. Thus he deliberately eliminated the old tribal units with their petty local tyrants and their continual feuds. Every year each of the new districts was obliged to provide food for the king and his household for one month.

Peace doubled the population to about eight hundred thousand people. As a result, new towns and cities had to be built to accommodate them and more land put under cultivation to feed the additional people. A farmer's calendar dating from about Solomon's reign was discovered at Gezer. It is a piece of soft limestone, only three by four inches in size, on which perhaps a schoolboy, writing in good Biblical Hebrew, inscribed eight lines. These list the farm work of each month of the year beginning in the fall. As translated by the archaeologist, William F. Albright, the verses run:

His two months are olive harvest   (Sept.-Nov.)
     His two months are planting grain,   (Nov.-Jan.)
          His two months are late planting;   (Jan.-Mar.)
His month is hoeing up of flax,   (Mar.-Apr.)
     His month is harvest of barley,   (Apr.-May)
          His month is harvest and feasting. (May-June)
His two months are vine-tending,   (June-Aug.)
          His month is summer fruit.   (Aug.Sept.)

The country's wealth brought prosperity to nobles, officials, landowners, and merchants, but the poor became poorer and class distinctions began to divide Israel. Eventually, when the huge costs of Solomon's army and his twenty-year building program exceeded his revenues, the king had to impose heavy taxes.

When he needed a dependable work force for his various undertakings, he conscripted thirty thousand men, each of whom was obliged to work three months for the king. To an independent people this "levy of forced labor out of all Israel" (1 Kings 5.13) was a repugnant burden, especially to farmers and craftsmen. Thus, despite great improvements in their living standards, the people felt that the loss of their freedom and human dignity for the sake of the glory of the state was intolerable. A revolt against Solomon, inspired by the prophet Ahijah, was led by a foreman of

the king's laborers, Jeroboam of the tribe of Ephraim.
Though this uprising was easily crushed, dangerous
discontent continued to spread. "Solomon sought therefore
to kill Jeroboam; but Jeroboam arose, and fled to Egypt, to
Shishak king of Egypt, and was in Egypt until the death of
Solomon" (1 Kings 11.40). In the next reign Jeroboam
would return and assume the role foreseen for him by the
prophet Ahijah.

From the political, social, economic, and religious
developments of the period of the united monarchy a new
national consciousness arose. Old beliefs were examined
and new ideas entertained; the old songs were sung and the
oral traditions rehearsed. The meaning of Israel's past and
her continuing relations with the Lord were interpreted
anew. Out of this creative ferment came Israel's first
literary flowering and the beginnings of the Bible. During
David's reign or soon thereafter appeared the historical
masterpiece mentioned above and known as the Early
Source of Samuel. This is the first extensive work of
history, and its author deserves to be called "the father of
history."

At this time the most influential literary and theological
achievement of Solomon's reign was written—the great
prose work known among scholars as the J Source of the
Pentateuch. It possibly underlies Joshua and Judges as well.
Its anonymous author is called the Yahwist because his
name for the deity was Yahweh. This writer combined
Israel's existing oral and written traditions in an extended
epic of universal history. In matchless literary form, the
Yahwist interpreted the history of Israel and her distinctive
faith so creatively and with such depth of understanding
that he profoundly influenced the prophets, priests, and
thinkers who came after him.

The Biblical account of Solomon, as was noted at the
beginning of this chapter, was not written during the

literary flowering of his reign, but was produced some four hundred years later by 6th-century historians. They judged the king's accomplishments and failures according to the later ideals of Deuteronomy and found him wanting. They wrote, "The Lord was angry with Solomon, because his heart had turned away from the Lord, the God of Israel" (1 Kings 11.9).

The king had indeed done injury to Israel's faith by transforming the Lord's people into a powerful, worldly state that was little different from the nations that surrounded her. Nevertheless, as time went on, most of the people forgot Solomon's burdensome taxes, his forced labor gangs, and his legacy of political upheaval, for they enjoyed remembering his "wisdom," his wealth, the architectural splendor of his Temple, and the king himself —"Solomon in all his glory" (Mt 6.29). In retrospect, his despotic, sophisticated reign appeared to have been a golden interval of prosperity and peace, when "Judah and Israel were as many as the sand by the sea; they ate and drank and were happy" (1 Kings 4.20).

Chapter 9 **Rehoboam Loses Half of the Kingdom**

c. 922 B.C.

1 Kings 12.1-20; 14.21-31;
2 Chronicles 10-12

Rehoboam, Solomon's arrogant and foolish son, succeeded his father. He immediately rejected the advice of his father's experienced counselors to heed the people's demand for relief from heavy taxation and forced labor. "My father made your yoke heavy, but I will add to your yoke," he threatened those who assembled at Shechem to confirm his kingship. "My father chastised you with whips, but I will chastise you with scorpions" (1 Kings 12.14).

With these reckless words Rehoboam destroyed the fragile political unity achieved by Saul, David, and Solomon. The northern tribes, unwilling to acknowledge a king who brazenly disregarded the wishes of his subjects, again raised the old cry of revolt first heard at Sheba's insurrection against David:

> "What portion have we in David?
>   We have no inheritance in the son of Jesse.
> To your tents, O Israel!
>   Look now to your own house, David,"
>
> 1 Kings 12.16

When the rebels stoned to death the official whom Rehoboam had sent to oversee the forced labor gangs, the king realized that he had indeed been repudiated. In haste, he mounted his chariot and fled from Shechem to the safety of his home in Jerusalem, while the northern states proclaimed the revolutionist Jeroboam as their king. He promptly established the capital of the new Kingdom of Israel at the ancient Hebrew center of Shechem.

The use of the name *Israel* indicates that the Northern Kingdom, in which the majority of Israelites lived, was accepted as the true Israel, while Judah, over which Rehoboam continued to reign, was regarded as the seceding state. In some periods Israel was called Ephraim, the name of the tribe to which Jeroboam belonged. Israel was also, at a later date, called Samaria from the name of its new capital city built by King Omri.

Judah and part of Benjamin, the only tribes that continued to be loyal to the house of David, comprised the Southern Kingdom of Judah. David's royal city of Jerusalem remained its capital. Two centuries later when the Northern Kingdom collapsed, the name *Israel* passed to Judah, for Israel was more than a political designation. As the prophets used it, the name stood for the whole people of Yahweh.

After the division of Solomon's kingdom, the vassal states of Moab and Ammon lingered for a while under Israel's control, but they soon joined other states that had won their independence. Thus the empire conquered by David disappeared and the united kingdom became two second-rate states. Never again did ancient Israel dominate the Middle East.

The history of the two Hebrew kingdoms recorded in 1 and 2 Kings covers a period of 335 years from the accession of Rehoboam to the final destruction of Jerusalem and the fall of Judah in 587 B.C. The record was compiled in the 6th century B.C. by historians who were guided by the ideals of Deuteronomy. They believed that national survival and prosperity resulted from loyalty and obedience to the

Lord. Consequently, they judged each king according to his loyalty to Yahweh and his zeal in stamping out idolatry and forbidding worship at shrines other than the Temple in Jerusalem.

Though the record of the nineteen kings of Israel and the twenty kings of Judah run concurrently in 1 and 2 Kings, the following sections deal with each kingdom separately, *Part Three* containing a sketch of Israel's rise and fall, and *Part Four*, the longer history of Judah.

The tentative chronology of this period follows the system developed by William F. Albright. The length of the individual reigns discussed below, however, is from *The Interpreter's Dictionary of the Bible*, and this sometimes differs from the number of years given in the Biblical text.

Part Three
Israel Rules in the North

Chapter 10 **Introduction to the Period**
c. 922-721 B.C.

Israel, during her two-hundred-year existence, enjoyed a few intervals of peace and prosperity, but her history was largely marked by dynastic struggles, social unrest, religious apostasy, wars against Judah, and repeated foreign invasions. The Northern Kingdom lacked the political stability that her southern neighbor, Judah, derived from being ruled by the royal line of David. In Israel, where the throne depended on the consent of the various tribes, there were repeated dynastic crises. Nine of her nineteen kings were usurpers, seven were assassinated, and one committed suicide.

In times of relative peace, trade flourished, Samaria and other cities were built, and the wealthy enjoyed considerable luxury. Improvement in the conditions of life for the prosperous, however, only widened the gap between rich and poor, increasing the hostility between classes. When small farmers fell into debt as a result of poor crops, they frequently lost not only their ancestral farms but also their personal freedom, for they and their children became slaves to rapacious creditors. In the face of such conditions the prophet Amos and his successors demanded social justice.

Israel lacked Judah's advantage in possessing the great religious center of Jerusalem. Moreover, Israel, because she was in closer contact with foreign religious influences than was Judah, more frequently adopted the beliefs and practices of neighboring peoples or ceased altogether to worship Yahweh. The evils of syncretism and apostasy were denounced by Israel's fiery prophet Elijah and his followers.

Friction constantly marred the relationship between the two Hebrew kingdoms. Border disputes often resulted in serious warfare whenever Israel or Judah widened the conflict by allying itself with neighboring states. Sometimes, however, a royal marriage or a common danger united both kingdoms in a temporary and uneasy alliance.

Because Israel was vulnerable on her northern and eastern frontiers, she was repeatedly invaded by the Aramean states of Syria. Frequently her land was ravaged, and her wealth drained by the tribute she was forced to pay in order to buy off invaders. Beyond Syria loomed the growing menace of Assyria, a predatory empire poised to conquer the entire East from Mesopotamia to the Nile and finally to engulf the Northern Kingdom of Israel.

The history of this period is recorded in 1 and 2 Kings by writers who believed, with the great prophets, that loyalty to Yahweh and obedience to the covenant insured prosperity, while repudiation of him resulted in national disaster. In the opinion of these historians, it was important that all worship be centered in the Temple in Jerusalem rather than in local shrines that were tainted with Canaanite nature worship. As none of the kings of Israel measured up to the historians' standards, they disapproved of them all. Many of the facts recorded in 1 and 2 Kings are confirmed by such inscriptions as those on the walls of the temple at Karnak, on a fragment of the Pharaoh Shishak's triumphal stele found at Megiddo, on the Moabite Stone, on the Black Obelisk of Shalmaneser III, and on the clay prism recording Sennacherib's reign.

Chapter 11 **Turmoil in the Northern Kingdom**

c. 922-876 B.C.

Jeroboam, Nadab, Baasha, Elah, Zimri

The Northern Kingdom's first half century witnessed political confusion, religious change, and external threats. Jeroboam (1 Kings 12.1-14.20; 2 Chron 10; 13) first established his capital at the old center of the tribal confederacy at Shechem, but later moved it six miles north to Tirzah.

His next concern was to provide sanctuaries in his own territory so that his people would not make yearly pilgrimages to Jerusalem's Temple in the heart of Rehoboam's Southern Kingdom. At Dan in the far north and at Bethel in the south, where Abraham had built an altar and Jacob had dreamed of angels, Jeroboam built two sanctuaries in which he placed the golden images of bull calves. He exhorted his subjects, "You have gone up to Jerusalem long enough. Behold your gods, O Israel" (1 Kings 12.28). Though "gods" should probably be translated "God," and though these animal images were doubtless merely substitutes for the cherubs that supported the invisible throne of Yahweh in Jerusalem's Temple, many people regarded them as an attempt to introduce the worship of the Canaanite bull that symbolized Baal. The author of 1 and 2 Kings viewed the setting up of the golden bulls and other acts of the king as sacrilegious and denounced Jeroboam for apostasy, saying, he "made Israel to sin" (1 Kings 14.16).

With Solomon's kingdom no longer strong and united, Pharoah Shishak took advantage of the weakness of the two successor kingdoms to invade Judah. Possibly he came at the suggestion of his former friend and vassal, Jeroboam (1 Kings 11.40), who surely welcomed the attack on Jerusalem, the stronghold of his enemy King Rehoboam. But Jeroboam's satisfaction must have turned to dismay when the Egyptian army did not halt at Judah's northern frontier, but invaded Israel itself and captured twenty of its towns. Though the Bible does not mention this raid, it is documented by two inscriptions, one carved on the north wall of the temple at Karnak, and the other on a fragment of Shishak's triumphal stele found at Megiddo.

After a reign of twenty-two years, Jeroboam died and was succeeded by his son Nadab (1 Kings 15.25-31). With him there began a long series of royal assassinations, for after reigning only a year Nadab was killed by the conspirator Baasha.

Baasha, of the tribe of Issachar (1 Kings 15.16-16.6; 2 Chron 16.1-6), assassinated not only Nadab, but all others of Jeroboam's family who might challenge his seizure of the throne of Israel. His twenty-four-year reign at Tirzah was marked by border warfare on two fronts: against Asa, king of Judah, in the south, and Ben-hadad, king of Syria, in the north.

The brief reign of his son Elah (1 Kings 16.8-14) ended at Tirzah in a drunken brawl during which the king was murdered by the conspirator Zimri, the commander of the king's chariotry.

Zimri (1 Kings 16.8-20) then usurped the throne, but remained in power only seven days. In that brief period, the Israelite army, which was then in the field, acclaimed their commander-in-chief, Omri, as king of Israel. He immediately marched to Tirzah and besieged the palace. Inside, Zimri set the building afire and perished in the flames.

Chapter 12 **The Dynasty of Omri**
c. 876-842 B.C.

Omri, (Tibni), Ahab,
Ahaziah, Jehoram

Omri (1 Kings 16.16-28) proved to be the strongest and most capable ruler of Israel and one whom the surrounding nations respected. Yet the historians of 1 Kings write, "Omri did what was evil in the sight of the Lord." They dismiss him and his politically important reign in twelve verses. First, Omri ended the civil war with which his reign began by defeating his rival army officer, Tibni, thus becoming undisputed king.

With statesmanlike ability he then developed his realm politically and economically. He chose the strategic hill of Samaria for his new capital and fortified it to withstand prolonged sieges. Against the growing threat of Assyria he concluded a defensive alliance with Israel's inveterate enemy, Syria. According to King Mesha's inscription on the Moabite Stone, which is now in the Louvre, Omri "humbled Moab many years" and imposed on it a heavy tribute of wool. He was the first king of Israel to maintain friendly relations with Judah. His trade arrangements with Ethbaal, the king of Tyre, were strengthened by the marriage of his son Ahab to the Tyrian princess Jezebel. During his twelve year reign, Omri earned the title of "David of the north," and his power so impressed the Assyrians that even after his death they called Israel "the land of Omri."

Ahab (1 Kings 16.29-22.40; 2 Chron 18) inherited from

his father a strong and thriving kingdom, which he continued to defend and advance economically for twenty years. Largely due to alliances with his wife's country of Tyre, trade between the two kingdoms flourished. Ahab completed the fortifications begun by Omri at Samaria and beautified its palaces. Here, during recent excavations of the hilltop site, archaeologists unearthed quantities of ivory objects, including wall panels and furniture inlays, all probably made by Tyrian or Phoenician craftsmen to decorate Ahab's "ivory house" (1 Kings 22.39).

Phoenician influence was not limited to trade and skilled craftsmanship. Jezebel, Ahab's notorious queen, fostered in Israel the worship of Baal and Asherah. Every day there dined at the queen's table hundreds of priests who served these Canaanite agricultural gods.

In this time of peril for Israel's faith, a man of God appeared, the fiery prophet Elijah, whose traditions and legends illuminate the history of Ahab's reign. The cycle of Elijah stories begins in 1 Kings 17 and dramatizes the basic conflict between, on one side, Israel's God, Yahweh, and his prophet Elijah, and on the other side, Baal and Asherah and their royal adherents, Ahab and Jezebel. The battle was first joined in the great drought that afflicted Israel.

"Is it you, you troubler of Israel?" demanded the king when the rugged prophet appeared before him.

> "It is not I who have troubled Israel," he replied, "but you and your father's family, by forsaking the commandments of the Lord and following Baal. But now, send and summon all Israel to meet me on Mount Carmel, and the four hundred and fifty prophets of Baal with them and the four hundred prophets of the goddess Asherah, who are Jezebel's pensioners."
>
> 1 Kings 18.17-19, NEB

On the wooded mountaintop of Carmel an altar was built and wood and the sacrifice placed upon it, but the wood was not lit. Then, with the people of Israel watching, Elijah challenged the prophets of Baal to a contest, saying,

> "You shall invoke your god by name and I will invoke the Lord by name; and the god who answers by fire, he is God." And all the people shouted their approval.
>
> 1 Kings 18.24, NEB

In vain the prophets of Baal called upon their god, but there was no answer. Next, Elijah came forward and prayed,

> "Lord God of Abraham, of Isaac, and of Israel, let it be known today that thou art God in Israel . . ." Then the fire of the Lord fell. It consumed the whole-offering, the wood, the stones, and the earth, and licked up the water in the trench. When all the people saw it, they fell prostrate, and cried, "The Lord is God, the Lord is God."
>
> 1 Kings 18.36, 38-39, NEB

At this moment, Israel's dangerous drift toward the gods of Canaan was checked as Elijah, the towering man of God, communicated to the people his awareness of the reality and power of the Lord. In the miraculous fire that Elijah called down from heaven, and in the rain that fell ending the long drought, Israel once again knew that, not Baal, but their God was indeed the supreme Lord of fire and rain and all the fertility of the earth.

In the 9th century, or later, perhaps inspired by a new national consciousness and a rebirth of the faith Elijah exemplified, a gifted writer of the Northern Kingdom appeared. He collected the oral story cycles that had long circulated in the north and from these traditional materials constructed the sacred history of Israel. This writer is called the Elohist because in his epic, before the period of Moses, he uses Elohim as the name for God. The narrative itself is designated as the E Source of the Pentateuch and other books. Scholars can distinguish it from the earlier J Source, with which it was later combined, not only by its use of Elohim rather than Yahweh, but also for its choice of subjects relating to the north. Its masterpiece is the story of the sacrifice of Isaac (Gen 22.1-13, 19).

Ahab's reign was marked by warfare. Only with Judah was there an interval of peace, promoted by the marriage of Athaliah, daughter of Ahab and Jezebel, to Jehoram, heir to the throne of Judah. On other fronts, war continued. Ahab's growing military strength enabled him to join a coalition of twelve petty kings, including his one-time enemy Ben-hadad of Syria. This coalition was formed to halt the westward advance of Shalmaneser III's Assyrian army, which, having set out from Nineveh, had already crossed the Euphrates and was only about a hundred and fifty miles north of Damascus at Qarqar. An inscription on the Black Obelisk of Shalmaneser III, now in the British Museum, states that battle between the allies and the Assyrians was joined at Qarqar on the Orontes in 853 B.C. In this battle Ahab commanded his ten thousand foot soldiers and two thousand chariots, which comprised half the coalition's chariotry. Though the inscription boasts that the Assyrian army crushed Ahab and his allies, the victory could hardly have been decisive, because for four years Shalmaneser failed to pursue his westward advance.

In this interval, with danger no longer threatening, the coalition fell apart. Ahab now attempted to recapture from his recent ally, Ben-hadad of Syria, the Hebrew city east of the Jordan called Ramoth-gilead. At this time the Syrians were occupying it in defiance of a treaty between the two countries. Aided by a Judean army led by King Jehoshaphat,

Ahab went into battle at Ramoth-gilead disguised as a common chariot soldier, for he feared Micaiah's prophecy that he would die (1 Kings 22.9-28). During the battle an arrow, fired at random, pierced the king's armor and gravely wounded him. Refusing to withdraw and thus risk the rout of his army, Ahab had himself "propped up in his chariot facing the Syrians until evening" (1 Kings 22.35). Then he died in his chariot and was taken to Samaria for burial.

Omri's dynasty ended with the reigns of Ahab's two sons. The elder was Ahaziah (1 Kings 22.51-2 Kings 1.18; 2 Chron 20.35-37), whom Elijah denounced for apostasy. One day the king fell through the latticed window of his upper chamber, became a cripple, and died childless after a two-year reign.

His brother Jehoram (Joram) (2 Kings 3.1-25; 9.14-26; 2 Chron 22.5-7) inherited troubles that had long been brewing. The miseries of the poor and the increasing wealth of the rich continued to undermine the social structure of Israel. These were the early years of the prophetic ministry of Elisha. Religious animosities between the followers of Yahweh and those of Baal had reached the breaking point. The army, demoralized by the long war against Syria and by Jehoram's weak leadership, was ready for revolt. After eight years, Jehoram's reign came to a violent end.

Chapter 13 **The Dynasty of Jehu**
c. 842-745 B.C.

Jehu, Jehoahaz, Jehoash,
Jeroboam II, Zechariah

While Jehu (2 Kings 9-10; 2 Chron 22.7-9) commanded the Israelite troops at Ramoth-gilead, a messenger from Elijah's successor, the prophet Elisha, suddenly appeared before him and anointed him king of Israel in the name of the Lord. The prophetic party, believing that Israel could never recover her political and religious liberty while Ahab's dynasty survived, commissioned Jehu to purge Israel of the evil of Ahab. With the help of the army, Jehu conspired to carry out a bloody *coup d'état*. He drove his chariot at a furious pace to the summer palace at Jezreel. There King Jehoram was recovering from battle wounds in the company of his nephew, King Ahaziah of Judah. Jehu assassinated both kings and had Jehoram's body cast into Naboth's vineyard. He ordered that the hated queen mother Jezebel be hurled from an upper window of the palace. Later, at Samaria, he had all claimants to Ahab's throne beheaded and all the priests of Baal murdered.

Jehu, having alienated Israel's former ally Phoenicia by the excesses of his revolution, turned to Assyria for help against his enemy Syria. The cost of this help, however, was tribute and submission. The Black Obelisk of Shalmaneser III portrays Jehu kneeling at the feet of the Assyrian conqueror while thirteen Israelites carry tribute. This is the only known contemporary representation of a king of either Israel or Judah.

After a reign of twenty-eight years, Jehu was succeeded by his son Jehoahaz (2 Kings 13.1-9). During his fifteen years as king, his army was destroyed by the Syrians and made "like the dust at threshing," while his kingdom became virtually subject to Syria.

When his son Jehoash (Joash) succeeded to the throne (2 Kings 13.9-25; 14.8-16; 2 Chron 25.17-24), he drove the Syrians back to their own borders and regained Israelite territories beyond the Jordan. In his sixteen-year reign, Jehoash also captured Jerusalem, despoiled the Temple, and reduced Judah to a vassal state. It remained, however, for Jehoash's son and successor, Jeroboam II, to achieve Israel's greatest measure of prosperity and power.

Jeroboam II (2 Kings 14.23-29; Amos 7.10-15), named for the first king of the Northern Kingdom, became, during his forty-one year reign, one of Israel's most successful kings. As usual, the authors of 2 Kings have little to say about him except that "he did what was evil in the sight of the Lord . . . and he made Israel to sin." His reign occurred at an auspicious period for Israel. To the south, Egypt was relatively weak. On Israel's northern border, Syria was fully occupied in fending off Assyrian encroachments. Thus Jeroboam was able to recover most of Israel's lost territory from Syria and to extend his frontiers farther than did any other king of the Northern Kingdom. An enlarged kingdom and freedom from warfare brought increased material prosperity to merchants, wealthy landowners, and officials, but failed to lift the burden of poverty and misery from small, independent farmers. This situation created a new chapter in Israel's religious development.

The event that gives prime importance to the long reign of Jeroboam II is the sudden appearance at Bethel of the passionate and fearless prophet Amos. Among his many predecessors were Nathan, Ahijah, Elijah, Elisha, and Micaiah, but Amos is the first whose collected words are preserved in the Bible. Though he came from Judah, from the mountaintop village of Tekoa south of Bethlehem, his message of doom was primarily addressed to the Northern Kingdom of Israel. At this time Judah and Israel were politically divided, but their inhabitants perceived themselves as the people of the covenant sharing the same glorious religious tradition.

Amos had been called to prophesy while herding his sheep and goats and tending the fruit of sycamore trees. "Go, prophesy to my people Israel" (Amos 7.15), the Lord commanded him. Obediently, he traveled more than twenty-five miles north to Israel's great royal shrine at Bethel. There the king's chief priest, Amaziah, roughly forbade him to prophesy. Nevertheless, Amos persisted and in ringing words delivered the Lord's judgments to throngs of people gathered at the sanctuary:

> For crime after crime of Israel
> > I will grant them no reprieve,
> because they sell the innocent for silver
> > and the destitute for a pair of shoes.
> They grind the heads of the poor into the earth
> > and thrust the humble out of their way . . . .
>
> Amos 2.6-7, NEB

His sermons were like trumpet calls to justice and righteousness, to right relations with other people and right relations with their Lord. The evils he denounced paint a picture of life during the time of Jeroboam II. There was drunkenness, gluttony, and immorality; luxury went hand in hand with senseless extravagance and stupid revelry; selfishness, callousness, and cruelty were destroying the social solidarity of the nation. Because judges were often bribed, the poor could not obtain justice. Merchants used false weights and demanded high prices for inferior goods (Amos 8.5-6). The sanctuaries were crowded and lavish sacrifices were offered, yet much of the piety seemed hollow. The Lord's voice was not heard, for the prophets had been silenced. All the elaborate ceremonies at the shrines were no substitute, Amos declared, for true worship and decent, upright living. In the Lord's name he proclaimed,

> "Even though you offer me your burnt offerings
>   and cereal offerings,
>   I will not accept them,
>
> •   •   •   •   •   •   •   •   •   •   •   •   •   •   •
>
> But let justice roll down like waters,
>   and righteousness like an ever-flowing stream."
>
>   Amos 5.22, 24

Justice, Amos believed, was the outstanding attribute of the Lord. Before it was too late, he exhorted the Israelites,

> Seek good and not evil,
>   that you may live,
> that the Lord of Hosts may be firmly on your side,
>   as you say he is.
>
>   Amos 5.14, NEB

They assumed that they were the Lord's own people, but Amos reminded them that this special privilege involved special obligations and responsibilities. He spoke in the Lord's words "to the whole nation which he brought up from Egypt:"

> For you alone have I cared
> among all the nations of the world;
> therefore will I punish you
>   for all your iniquities.
>
>   Amos 3.1-2, NEB

After the death of Jeroboam II, catastrophy overtook Israel. Jehu's dynasty finally ended, as it had begun, in bloodshed. Jeroboam's son Zechariah (2 Kings 15.8-12), after a reign of only six months, was assassinated by the conspirator Shallum who was then proclaimed king.

Chapter 14 **The Last Kings of Israel**

c. 745-721 B.C.

Shallum, Menahem, Pekahiah,
Pekah, Hoshea

Revolts and counter-revolts produced anarchy as the assassination of one weak and brutal ruler now followed another. In the northeast, Assyria under Tiglath-pileser III was poised for conquest. After only a month in power, the assassin, Shallum (2 Kings 15.10-15), was himself assassinated by Menahem (2 Kings 15.14-22). With the help of the Assyrians, whom Menahem appeased with a tribute of a thousand talents of silver extracted from wealthy landowners, he managed to remain king for seven years. His son and successor, Pekahiah (2 Kings 15.22-26), was murdered after a two-year reign by the anti-Assyrian party led by Pekah, the army commander. This rapid succession of kings is alluded to in Hosea's prophecies.

> They made kings, but not through me.
> They set up princes, but without my knowledge.

Again the Lord declared,

> All their kings are fallen;
> and none of them calls upon me.

Hosea 8.4; 7.7

Hosea, a native of Israel, began to prophesy at the end of the reign of Jeroboam II and continued probably to the accession of Hoshea, whose name the prophet shared.

Because of the nation's exposed position in the path of
Assyria's thrust toward Egypt, Israel had little chance to
survive politically. Yet Hosea, even in this perilous situation, dared to hope, for he was convinced of the reality of
God's love for his people.

> When Israel was a child, I loved him,
> 	and out of Egypt I called my son.
> The more I called them,
> 	the more they went from me.
>
> Hosea 11.1-2

Hosea clearly stated what the Lord desired from the
people whom he loved, his people of the covenant. He did
not want their empty forms of worship, but the love that
springs from minds that know and hearts that are loyal.

> For I desire steadfast love and not sacrifice,
> 	the knowledge of God, rather than burnt
> 		offerings.
>
> Hosea 6.6

Like Amos, Hosea perceived Israel's situation.

> Hear the word of the Lord, O Israel;
> for the Lord has a charge to bring against the people of
> 		the land:
> 	There is no good faith or mutual trust,
> 	no knowledge of God in the land,
> oaths are imposed and broken, they kill and rob;
> 	there is nothing but adultery and licence,
> 	one deed of blood after another.
> 	Therefore the land shall be dried up,
> 	and all who live in it shall pine away . . .
>
> Hosea 4.1-3, NEB

Out of the tragic experience of his own marriage, Hosea reached his deepest insight. He understood that the purpose of God's judgment against Israel was not vengeance and destruction, but healing and redemption.

> I will not execute my fierce anger,
>> I will not again destroy Ephraim;
> for I am God and not man,
>> the Holy One in your midst,
>> and I will not come to destroy.

> Hosea 11.9

Despite the heroic attempts of the prophets to change Israel's course before it was too late, Israel's history moved inexorably toward disaster. After his seizure of the throne, Pekah (2 Kings 15.25-31; 2 Chron 28.6) was powerless to halt Assyria's rapid advance under Tiglath-pileser III. The Assyrian king captured Syria, annexed much of Israel, and, exercising his ruthless policy of exterminating nations to enlarge his empire, he uprooted many Galileans and resettled them in Assyria.

The instability characteristic of Israel's kingship again became evident in Pekah's assassination in a conspiracy led by Hoshea (2 Kings 15.30; 17.1-6). Hoshea then made himself king and reigned for nine years as the last king of Israel. Tiglath-pileser III required Hoshea to pay heavy tribute in gold and silver talents, but after the Assyrian conqueror's death in 727 B.C., Hoshea refused to send the intolerable levy to his successor, Shalmaneser V. Thereupon, a new Assyrian army invaded Israel, imprisoned Hoshea, and laid siege to the city of Samaria. For three years the hilltop capital, built and heavily fortified by Omri a century and a half earlier, resisted its attacker.

Finally, in 721 B.C. Samaria fell to the Assyrian army of the new king, Sargon II. In his annals Sargon boasts of conquering "the wide land of Omri" and taking 27,290 Israelites to Assyria as captives. The deported Israelites, subsequently referred to as the "Ten Lost Tribes of Israel" (though ten distinct tribes no longer existed), were absorbed by the peoples among whom they settled and disappeared from history. With their disappearance the Northern Kingdom of Israel ceased to exist.

The great majority of the Israelites, however, remained in their own land and intermarried with settlers whom the conquerors brought in from Babylonia and Syria. This was the origin of the racially and culturally mixed people known as the Samaritans. Though their religion, like Judah's, was based on the Pentateuch, they became antagonistic toward Judah. Two hundred years later, in the Persian period, they opposed the restoration of the Temple in Jerusalem and the rebuilding of the city walls by Nehemiah. Later still, Samaritan hostility toward the Jews was encountered by Jesus (John 4.9).

Part Four
Judah Rules in the South

Chapter 15 **Introduction to the Period**
c. 922-587 B.C.

When the northern tribes of Israel seceded from the united kingdom that Rehoboam had inherited from Solomon, his father, only Judah and part of little Benjamin remained loyal to the dynasty of their old hero David. Nevertheless, the small size and the relative isolation of Judah in the highlands of Palestine were more of an advantage than a drawback, for they enabled her people to stay out of the power struggles that engulfed the larger and more prosperous states of the Middle East during most of the next two centuries. Judah fortunately possessed Jerusalem, the royal city of David, thus providing the Southern Kingdom with a secure political capital and the center for the people's worship. Moreover, the dynasty of David provided a comparatively stable succession to the throne and the advantage of several long reigns. In her 335-year history, Judah had twenty rulers, while Israel, in existence for only 201 years, had nineteen. Not only did Israel's political upheavals react upon Judah, but constant friction between the two sister states weakened their ability to defend themselves against the aggressive powers of the region.

Chapter 16   **Rehoboam and His Heirs**
c. 922-842 B.C.

Rehoboam, Abijam, Asa, Jehoshaphat,
Jehoram, Ahaziah

Rehoboam (1 Kings 12.1-24; 14.21-31; 2 Chron 10-12) inherited from his father the largest and strongest kingdom the Hebrews ever ruled. Unfortunately he did not inherit the shrewdness and judgment of his father and grandfather, so, from the day he failed to put down the uprising in the north and fled in his chariot from Shechem to Jerusalem, he found himself, as we have noted, ruling a drastically reduced state. Even this was insecure, for Jeroboam of Israel constantly threatened his northern border, making it necessary for Rehoboam to fortify his frontier towns.

At the beginning of his reign, Rehoboam faced a new threat from the south, possibly one that caused his sudden flight from Shechem. Egypt, which had been politically dormant, roused to action under the aggressive new Pharaoh Shishak, whose ambition it was to restore to Egypt her Asiatic empire. In c. 918 B.C. Shishak's army swept through Philistia, Edom, and Judah, plundering Jerusalem's royal treasures and the shields of gold with which Solomon had decorated the Temple. This raid greatly weakened Judah.

The Davidic line of kings continued, after Rehoboam's death, in the three-year reign of his son Abijam (Abijah) (1 Kings 15.1-8; 2 Chron 13.1-14.1). Abijam struggled against Israel and succeeded in enlarging his kingdom by the annexation of the territory of Benjamin.

Abijam's son Asa (1 Kings 15.8-24; 2 Chron 14-16) reigned for forty-one years, beginning during Jeroboam's reign in Israel and lasting to Omri's. Because the conflict between Judah and Israel continued, Asa offered King Benhadad of Damascus a bribe of the Temple treasures in return for his help against Israel. This enabled Asa to extend Judah's territory northward at Israel's expense. According to the Biblical historians, Asa "did what was right in the eyes of the Lord" (1 Kings 15.11) and tried to reform religion by abolishing the cultic objects introduced by the Canaanites. His reform extended even to the royal household and included his mother, Maacah, whom he deposed from the position of queen mother because she had set up a shrine to Asherah, the goddess of fertility.

The long reign of Asa was followed by his son Jehoshaphat's twenty-five years as king (1 Kings 22.1-50; 2 Chron 17.1-21.1). During these fairly peaceful and prosperous years, Jehoshaphat introduced religious and political reforms. He ended the chronic hostility between Judah and Israel by uniting the two kingdoms against Syria and by arranging the marriage of his son and heir, Jehoram, to the princess Athaliah, daughter of King Ahab and his queen, Jezebel. This alliance with the dynasty that had introduced Baal-worship into Israel outraged many in Judah who were loyal to Yahweh.

When Jehoshaphat's son Jehoram (Joram) (2 Kings 8.16-24; 2 Chron 21) came to the throne, he lost his authority over Edom and with it control of the southern trade routes. In Chronicles he is said to have murdered his six brothers and some of the princes of Israel as well, possibly to put down their rebellion against him. His reign lasted only eight years.

Ahaziah, Jehoram's son (2 Kings 8.25-9.28; 2 Chron 22.1-9), succeeded his father. During his first year in power, he allied himself with his uncle, King Jehoram of Israel.

While paying a friendly visit to his uncle at Jezreel, both kings were attacked and murdered by Jehu, the revolutionary, who having arrived swiftly in his chariot, took both kings by surprise. Jehoram died immediately, but Ahaziah, mortally wounded, died later at Megiddo.

Chapter 17 Queen Athaliah Usurps the Throne

c. 842-837 B.C.

After the assassination of her son Ahaziah, the queen mother Athaliah (2 Kings 11; 2 Chron 22.10-23.15) seized the throne of Judah and reigned over the Southern Kingdom for six years. She was the only queen to reign over either Judah or Israel. As daughter of Ahab and Jezebel and a granddaughter both of Omri of Israel and Ethbaal of Tyre, she belonged to the Israelite and Tyrian royal families, not to the house of David. Her first act as queen was to eliminate the royal line of David. In this she was not entirely successful, because her grandson Jehoash, the six-month-old son of the murdered king, was rescued with his nurse from the wholesale massacre of the royal family by Jehosheba, his father's half-sister. Throughout Athaliah's reign, Jehosheba, as the wife of the high priest Johoiada, was able to keep her nephew hidden in the Temple precincts while her husband carefully planned an uprising against the hated queen.

When the young prince reached the age of seven, his uncle, with the support of the Temple guard, brought Jehoash out of hiding and crowned him king of Judah to the acclamation of the people of Jerusalem. Hearing the blowing of the ceremonial trumpets, Queen Athaliah went to the Temple where her grandson stood by the pillar in the midst of the rejoicings. "Treason! Treason!" she cried as she rent her clothes. The soldiers under Johoiada's orders seized the queen and dragged her outside the precincts of the Temple before putting her to death.

Chapter 18 **A Century of Independence**
c. 837-735 B.C.

Jehoash, Amaziah, Uzziah,
Jotham

During the early part of the forty-year reign of Jehoash
(Joash) (2 Kings 11.21-12.21; 2 Chron 24), his uncle, the
high priest Johoiada, acted as regent. He succeeded in
freeing Judah from the Phoenician or Tyrian religion and
culture that had been introduced by Athaliah. After the
young king assumed power for himself, he instituted an
honest system of collecting revenue for the Temple, which
was then in need of extensive repairs. When the Syrians,
led by Hazael, swept south along the Philistine coast and
threatened to occupy Jerusalem, Jehoash bought them off
by paying tribute of all the golden treasures of the Temple
and the palace. A band of the king's officers, doubtless
angered by this national humiliation, which they blamed
upon the king's policy of appeasing the Syrians, assassinated
Jehoash in his palace.

Amaziah (2 Kings 14.1-20; 2 Chron 25), the son of
Jehoash, executed his father's assassins, but, in an act of
clemency that was unusual at this time, he spared the children of the assassins (2 Kings 14.6). During his eighteen-year
reign, Amaziah reoccupied Edom. Elated by this victory,
he challenged the Israelites to battle at Beth-shemesh where
he suffered defeat. As a result, Jerusalem was captured, its
walls partially demolished, the Temple again plundered,
and Amaziah himself taken prisoner. He was probably
deposed during his absence, for on returning from captivity

to Jerusalem, Amaziah found his enemies in control and fled to Lachish where his opponents conspired to murder him.

His son Uzziah (Azariah) (2 Kings 14.21-22; 15.1-7; 2 Chron 26), proclaimed king at the age of sixteen, enjoyed a stable reign of forty-one years (fifty-two years according to the Bible reckoning) most of which coincided with the forty-year reign of Jeroboam II of Israel. During this long period Judah reached the height of its power and prosperity. At this time Egypt was in eclipse, Assyrian aggression was temporarily halted, and the Syrians were weak. By his conquests in Philistia, Uzziah gained control over important trade routes. His military success against the frontier tribes to the east gave him control over the caravan routes from Arabia as well as those through Edom, and thus enabled him to re-establish the port of Elath on the Gulf of Aqaba. He reorganized the army, rebuilt Jerusalem's walls, erected watch towers throughout Judah, and constructed cisterns to store water for irrigation. He himself "had large herds, both in the Shephelah and in the plain, and he had farmers and vinedressers in the hills and in the fertile lands, for he loved the soil" (2 Chron 26.10).

His wise economic and agricultural policies during this interval of peace made him so strong that he assumed leadership of the alliance of western states against Assyria. In his later years he contracted leprosy and, because of his ritual uncleanness, had to live in isolation. Nevertheless, until his death he remained the power behind the throne during the eight-year regency of his son Jotham, whose own reign lasted only eight years (2 Kings 15.32-38; 2 Chron 27).

The year Uzziah died and Jotham finally succeeded him was c. 742 B.C., a year notable in history for Isaiah's vision in the Temple. The old king's death had caused a sense of uncertainty and foreboding among the people that must

have been shared by a sensitive young city man like Isaiah.
He was undoubtedly aware of the prophetic messages of
Amos and Hosea in Israel and, like them, disturbed by the
nation's reliance on material wealth and military might. In
both Israel and Judah the correct sacrifices continued to be
offered, but the majority of the people no longer put their
trust in the Lord, their King. Isaiah may have been one of
the priests assisting in the splendid ceremonies inside
Jerusalem's Temple when, one day, he was swept up in an
overpowering experience of the reality and majesty, the
power and holiness, of the Lord. In his own words, he
reports that moment of transcendence.

> . . . I saw the Lord sitting upon a throne, high and
> lifted up; and his train filled the temple. Above him
> stood the seraphim . . . . And one called to another
> and said:
>
> > "Holy, holy, holy is the Lord of hosts;
> > the whole earth is full of his glory."
>
> And the foundations of the thresholds shook at the
> voice of him who called, and the house was filled with
> smoke.
>
> Isaiah 6.1-4

His first reaction to the sublime and awesome holiness of
God was a sense of his own human sinfulness, and he cried,

> "Woe is me! For I am lost; for I am a man of unclean
> lips, and I dwell in the midst of a people of unclean
> lips; for my eyes have seen the King, the Lord of
> hosts!"
>
> Isaiah 6.5

Forgiven, purified, and made holy by the touch of the
seraph's burning coal to his lips, Isaiah heard the Lord

challenge him and say, "Whom shall I send, and who will go for us?" In this hour of decision Isaiah knew what he must do, "Here am I! Send me!" he cried.

During the next forty years, while Judah, under the kings Jotham, Ahaz, Hezekiah, and Manasseh, moved inexorably from one political crisis to another toward eventual disaster, Isaiah spoke as a prophet for the Lord, interpreting His will and purpose for the people of Judah and continually searching to discover His laws.

> With all my heart I long for thee in the night,
> I seek thee eagerly when dawn breaks;
> for, when thy laws prevail in the land,
> the inhabitants of the world learn justice.
>
> Isaiah 26.9, NEB

Isaiah was neither a dreamy mystic nor a fortuneteller. Prophecy in Israel and Judah was not "history written beforehand." Like the other prophets, Isaiah was a practical man involved in the issues of his own day. But he was also fired with a vision of the reality and holiness of God and inspired to proclaim this vision in the context of the world he knew. His task was heartbreaking. The kings whom he advised lived in fear and were governed by worldly considerations, and the people lacked understanding because their ears were insensitive and their eyes shut against the Lord.

Chapter 19 **Struggles for National Survival**
c. 735-609 B.C.

Ahaz, Hezekiah, Manasseh,
Amon, Josiah

Ahaz (2 Kings 16; Isa 7.1-9; 2 Chron 27-28) was twenty years old when he acceded to the throne of his father, Jotham. At first, because he felt secure in the relative isolation of Judah's mountainous country, he refused to join the coalition formed by Pekah of Israel and Rezin of Damascus against the advancing power of Assyria. These two allies, angered by his rejection of their offer, marched south against Jerusalem and threatened to depose young Ahaz and to place a puppet king of their own choice on Judah's throne. With this threat hanging over him and the presence of two armies on his soil, Ahaz's "heart and the heart of his people shook as the trees of the forest shake before the wind" (Isa 7.2).

At this moment Isaiah, accompanied by his little son, went out to meet the anxious king "at the end of the conduit of the upper pool." Ahaz was probably there to inspect Jerusalem's water supply in case his enemies laid siege to the city. The prophet advised the king not to join in the power struggles of the region or to ask Assyria to intervene against his two enemy states, but to have faith in the Lord. "Take heed, be quiet, do not fear, and do not let your heart be faint because of these two smoldering stumps of firebrands" (Isa 7.4), exhorted Isaiah in the Lord's name. In this forceful image he referred to the kings of Israel and Damascus whom the prophet perceived as more troublesome than dangerous. Then he added, "Have firm faith, or you will not stand firm" (Isa 7.9, NEB).

Ahaz, because his faith was weak, brushed aside Isaiah's advice and his assurance that God would send a sign— Immanuel, "God with us" (Isa 7.14). The king preferred to put his trust in his own political wisdom and in the military strength of the Assyrian army. Accordingly, to gain Assyrian help against Syria and Israel, Ahaz sent to Tiglath-pileser III, the Assyrian king, an enormous bribe of gold and silver from the Temple and from his own royal treasury.

Tiglath-pileser, undoubtedly pleased to be paid for what he planned to do in any case, attacked Israel in 732 B.C. In that unhappy country Pekah was killed by Hoshea, who then ascended the throne.

By unwisely enlisting Tiglath-pileser's help against his enemies, Ahaz made Judah a tribute-paying vassal of Assyria. His submission involved religious as well as political affairs and probably obliged Ahaz to set up in Yahweh's Temple in Jerusalem an altar to Ashur, the Assyrian god whom Tiglath-pileser worshiped. This act of apostasy, which was to have serious consequences for Judah's national life, was condemned by the historians who wrote Kings and Chronicles and by the prophet Isaiah.

Ahaz's policy of submission to Assyria, however, enabled Judah, after Israel's capital city of Samaria fell in 721 B.C. and Israel herself ceased to exist, to escape her sister kingdom's fate. Judah's survival made her a refuge for fugitives from the north who brought with them their traditions and literature, especially the Elohist's history of Israel known as the E Source of the Pentateuch. Thus, much of the religious heritage that would otherwise have been lost was preserved.

During the sixteen-year reign of Ahaz, there lived in the country village of Moresheth, twenty-five miles southwest of Jerusalem, a younger contemporary of Amos, Hosea, and Isaiah—the peasant prophet Micah. Like the other great prophets of that century, Micah denounced the social injustice suffered by the poor and oppressed among whom he lived. He became a fierce prophet of doom who predicted the fall of Jerusalem and preached of divine judgment, but he looked forward to the Lord's forgiveness and a future restoration of the Lord's people. In a single classic sentence, Micah sums up the message of all the prophets concerning God's justice and love and the need for humble faith and ethical living:

> and what does the Lord require of you
> but to do justice, and to love kindness,
> and to walk humbly with your God?

> Micah 6.8

Hezekiah (2 Kings 18-20; Isa 36-39; 2 Chron 29-32), Ahaz's son and successor, reigned for twenty-nine years. He was a capable and energetic king in contrast to his weak and subservient father. He reversed his father's policy of submission to Assyria, removed the symbols of the Assyrian cult from the Temple, and, with the encouragement of the prophets Micah and Isaiah, attempted to purify religion from pagan defilement in order to restore the true worship of Yahweh. His purpose was to revive the glories of his ancestor David's reign. To that end he encouraged building and trade. He also made preparations for war and gave his engineers the task of providing Jerusalem with a dependable supply of water in case of a siege.

Their problem was to bring water from the Spring of Gihon, which was outside the city walls, into a new reservoir called the Pool of Siloam inside the walls. To do this it was necessary to bore through solid rock. Two groups of stonecutters started from opposite ends and, using hand picks, tunneled towards each other. One of the oldest known Hebrew inscriptions was found near the Siloam end. In classical Hebrew it celebrates the success of this engineering feat: ". . . While the workmen were still lifting pick to pick, each toward his neighbor, and while three cubits remained to be cut through, each heard the voice of the other who called his neighbor . . . . And on the day of the boring through the stonecutters struck, each to meet his fellow, pick to pick; and there flowed the waters into the pool. . . ."

The tunnel they bored is nearly a third of a mile long and in places only twenty inches wide. Its average height is six feet. Today it is one of Jerusalem's most impressive monuments to Judah's resolve to defend herself against Assyria during the reign of Hezekiah. In a dry season and with a guide, an adventurous visitor, undeterred by mud, wet feet, or a long, dark, twisting tunnel, can today wade through its channel from end to end.

Hezekiah, in defiance of mighty Assyria, allied himself with both Egypt and the provinces of the Assyrian empire that were in revolt against their new king, Sennacherib. He had succeeded his father, Sargon II, in 704 B.C. Isaiah, as he had once counseled Ahaz, now warned his son urging Hezekiah not to join the rebellion. Because of his conviction that the Lord is Sovereign over all nations, the prophet exhorted the king to trust in the Lord and patiently await deliverance, saying,

> For thus said the Lord God, the Holy One of Israel,
>> "In returning and rest you shall be saved;
>> in quietness and in trust shall be your strength."
>>> Isaiah 30.15

The prophet's advice was not taken and events moved swiftly to a conclusion.

The Assyrian emperor first put down the general revolt of his subject province, defeating Hezekiah's allies one by one. Sennacherib then continued south with his army to deal with Judah. In Lord Byron's words,

> The Assyrian came down like the wolf on the fold,
> And his cohorts were gleaming in purple and gold.

Forty-six of Judah's fortified cities were besieged and conquered and many Judeans captured. Hezekiah himself was trapped in Jerusalem, "like a bird in a cage," boasted Sennacherib in his royal Annals. These are inscribed in cuneiform on a six-sided clay cylinder found at Nineveh and now in the British Museum. After forcing Hezekiah to pay a crushing tribute, the Assyrians suddenly withdrew from the siege of Jerusalem. Judah, though devastated, escaped the complete destruction that had been brought upon Israel twenty years earlier. Isaiah's assurances to the king (Isa 37.5-7, 30-35) and his trust in the Lord were triumphantly vindicated. His prophecies that a "remnant" of Judah would return to the Lord (Isa 10.20-21; 37.30-32) were long remembered.

It is unclear whether the sudden withdrawal of the Assyrians was due to an outbreak of bubonic plague in Sennacherib's army, to a rebellion in Babylon compelling him to recall his troops, or to his judgment that he had spent enough time punishing Judah. The little country was left nominally independent, but its condition is graphically revealed by Isaiah:

> Your country lies desolate,
>   your cities are burned with fire;
> in your very presence
>   aliens devour your land.
>
>   Isaiah 1.7

Manasseh (2 Kings 21.1-18; 2 Chron 33.1-20), Hezekiah's young son and successor, soon became the vassal of Sennacherib and remained subject to Assyria throughout his forty-five-year reign, the longest in Judah's history. To the record in 2 Kings, Chronicles adds that Manasseh was seized by the Assyrian army (perhaps due to an attempted revolt on his part), bound in fetters, and deported to Babylon. There he repented, prayed to God, and was restored to his throne. The Prayer of Manasseh in the Apocrypha supplements this tradition. Undoubtedly because Manasseh remained politically dependent on Assyria, he was obliged to restore the Assyrian religious practices his father had been able to abolish. He introduced the worship of the sun, moon, and stars, set up local sanctuaries for the rituals of Baal and Asherah, and tolerated human sacrifice, even sacrificing his own son. The prophets bitterly condemned the king for thus dishonoring the pure religion of the Lord, and his apostasy earned for him the reputation of being Judah's most wicked king. In Rabbinic literature there is a tradition that the prophet Isaiah suffered martyrdom in Manasseh's reign.

Manassah's policy of subservience to Assyria, however, made it possible for little Judah in her mountainous area to stay out of the violent conflicts of the region and enjoy four decades of peace. During this period the Assyrian Empire reached the height of its power and extent. Sennacherib's heir, Esarhaddon, began the conquest of Egypt. Finally, Sennacherib's grandson, the mighty Ashurbanipal, who was a general as well as a patron of arts and letters and the last great emperor of Assyria, ruled from his capital of Nineveh. His diverse realm included the entire Fertile Crescent and extended from Susa near the Persian Gulf to Sardis in Asia Minor, and south to Thebes in Egypt.

In Judah, Amon (2 Kings 21.18-26; 2 Chron 33.20-25) succeeded his father Manasseh, but reigned only two years as an Assyrian puppet king before being assassinated in a palace conspiracy.

Josiah, Amon's eight-year-old son (2 Kings 21.24-23.30; 2 Chron 34-35), was placed on the throne by "the people of the land." During Ashurbanipal's last years, while Assyria was beginning to disintegrate from inner weakness and civil war, its authority over Judah decreased. This gave Josiah freedom to repudiate the gods of Assyria and, as early as the eighth year of his reign, "to seek the God of David his father" (2 Chron 34.3). He even dreamed of restoring David's old empire and to that end he quietly extended his power as far north as Galilee (Naphtali), into provinces lately dominated by Assyria (2 Chron 34.6-7).

One of the most dramatic events of Josiah's reign occurred in 621 B.C. while the Temple was undergoing repairs to make it fit for the worship of the Lord. A scroll was found in the sacred precincts and when the high priest put it in the hands of Shaphan, the king's secretary, he announced, "I have found the book of the law in the house of the Lord" (2 Kings 22.8). After the scroll was read to Josiah he rose and, in the ancient gesture of sorrow and remorse, rent his clothes, saying, ". . . great is the wrath of the Lord that is kindled against us, because our fathers have not obeyed the words of this book, to do according to all that is written concerning us" (2 Kings 22.13). Next, the scroll was taken to the prophetess Huldah, who pronounced the "book of the law" to be an authentic expression of the will of God. At length, the king summoned "all the people, both small and great" and read the scroll to them. Thereupon, with great solemnity both king and people renewed the covenant that six hundred years earlier, in the days of Moses, their ancestors had ratified in the wilderness. Once again they affirmed the holiness and divine destiny of the people of Israel:

> And the king stood by the pillar and made a covenant
> before the Lord, to walk after the Lord and to keep his
> commandments, and his testimonies and his statutes,
> with all his heart and all his soul, to perform the
> words of this covenant that were written in this book;
> and all the people joined in the covenant.
>
> 2 Kings 23.3

The book that largely set in motion Josiah's religious reformation is now thought to have been an early edition of Deuteronomy consisting of chapters 12 to 26. Its message, which had doubtless been in quiet preparation during the years of apostasy and persecution that marked Manasseh's reign, came to light only when Josiah set Judah free from the Assyrian cult. For the first time in Hebrew history, a written authority recalled the nation to its great traditions and demonstrated that divine punishment inevitably follows evil-doing. A book was now considered as valid as a prophetic message and the idea of the Bible was born.

According to the precepts of "the book of the law," Josiah abolished foreign cults, destroyed local shrines, made Jerusalem the center of public worship, and declared that the social and moral laws of Moses were to be the law of Judah. These measures helped to re-establish Judah as the people of God, but the idolatry of the previous reigns was too deeply entrenched to be entirely swept away by Josiah's reforms.

In the early years of Josiah's reign, before the king had begun to purify the worship in the Temple, the prophet Zephaniah had attacked the corrupt religious practices introduced during the time of Manasseh and Amon. Zephaniah was a young aristocrat of Jerusalem, who, like the king, claimed descent from King Hezekiah. He accused the important people of Jerusalem—officials, judges, prophets, and priests alike—of unrighteousness and lack of faith. Because Judah had rebelled against her God, the day

of her punishment was fast approaching. He called it "the
day of the wrath of the Lord." It would be "a day of
distress and anguish, a day of ruin and devastation, a day
of darkness and gloom, a day of clouds and thick darkness,
a day of trumpet blast and battle cry against the fortified
cities . . ." (Zeph 1.15-16). In this crisis the prophet called
upon a remnant of the people to repent and return to the
Lord:

> Seek the Lord, all you humble of the land,
>   who do his commands;
> seek righteousness, seek humility;
>   perhaps you may be hidden
>   on the day of the wrath of the Lord.
>
> Zephaniah 2.3

Undoubtedly Zephaniah supported Josiah's reforms, as
did young Jeremiah, the second great prophet of this
period. Jeremiah exhorted the people to "hear the words of
this covenant and do them" (Jer 11.6). Later, however,
Jeremiah perceived that the reforms sprang largely from
political motives rather than from a genuine change of
heart, and that the people needed more than reformed
worship, and more than formal assent to the laws of God.
The prophet believed that a spiritual rebirth must take
place in the depth of each person's being, a rebirth that
would create a new relationship with the Lord:

> "Behold, the days are coming, says the Lord, when I
> will make a new covenant with the house of Israel and
> the house of Judah . . . . I will put my law within
> them, and I will write it upon their hearts; and I will
> be their God, and they shall be my people. And . . .
> they shall all know me, from the least of them to the
> greatest, says the Lord. . . ."
>
> Jeremiah 31.31-34

Near the end of Josiah's thirty-one-year reign, the Assyrian empire, whose savage might had been feared and hated from the Euphrates to the Nile, collapsed quickly. The Chaldeans, a desert tribe that had come to power in Babylon, joined with the Medes, an Indo-European people from the mountains south of the Caspian Sea. Their combined forces besieged and captured Nineveh in 612 B.C. The Hebrew poet and prophet Nahum, in his graphic ode celebrating the city's fall, wrote,

> Woe to the bloody city,
>> all full of lies and booty—
> no end to the plunder!
> •　　•　　•　　•　　•　　•　　•
> All who hear the news of you
>> clap their hands over you.
> For upon whom has not come
>> your unceasing evil?
>
> Nahum 3.1, 19

In the midst of the international turmoil of the time, Josiah unwisely led his army north to Megiddo to protect his newly annexed northern territories. This conflicted with the plans of Pharaoh Neco II to re-establish Egyptian political control over Syria and Palestine. In the ensuing encounter at Megiddo, Josiah was wounded and carried in his chariot back to Jerusalem where he died. With his death Judah lost her independence and became a vassal of Egypt.

Jeremiah, in his oracle concerning three of Josiah's successors, paid tribute to Josiah in words addressed to his sons:

> Did not your father eat and drink
>> and do justice and righteousness?
>> Then it was well with him.
> He judged the cause of the poor and needy;
>> then it was well.
> Is not this to know me?
>> says the Lord.
>
> Jeremiah 22.15-16

Chapter 20 **The Fall of Judah**
609-587 B.C.

Jehoahaz, Jehoiakim, Jehoiachin,
Zedekiah

Judah's last four kings, three of them sons of Josiah and one his grandson, reigned as virtual puppets of the two great powers that succeeded Assyria as masters of the Middle East: first Egypt, and later the New Babylonian Empire of the Chaldeans.

Jehoahaz (Shallum) (2 Kings 23.30-34; 2 Chron 36.1-4; Jer 22.10-11) succeeded his father Josiah, but ruled only three months before Pharaoh Neco II summoned him to appear at the Egyptian camp, deposed him, and took him as a prisoner to Egypt where he died.

The Egyptians then made his brother Eliakim king and gave him the throne name of Jehoiakim (2 Kings 23.34-24.6; 2 Chron 36.4-8). Jehoiakim ruled despotically for eleven years as a vassal king of Egypt. Though Judah was severely weakened by the heavy tribute Egypt imposed on the people, Jehoiakim increased their already heavy burdens by building a luxurious palace for himself with forced labor. In one of his oracles the prophet Jeremiah rebuked the king for this structure, saying, "Woe to him who builds his house by unrighteousness . . ." (Jer 22.13-17). A scroll of Jeremiah's prophecies warning Judah of her impending punishment was read to Jehoiakim one day as he sat in his winter palace. With no respect for the word of God, the king slashed off the columns as they were read and threw them into a fire burning in his brazier until the entire scroll was consumed (Jer 36.20-31).

During Jehoiakim's reign, Pharaoh Neco II was decisively defeated at Carchemish on the upper Euphrates in 605 B.C. by the Babylonian crown prince, Nebuchadnezzar—an overthrow that freed Judah from Egyptian domination only to subject her to Babylonian control.

At this time of evil abroad and wickedness within Judah, the prophet Habakkuk raised a despairing cry and asked,

> O Lord, how long shall I cry for help,
>   and thou wilt not hear?
> . . . .
> why dost thou look on faithless men,
>   and art silent when the wicked swallows up
>   the man more righteous than he?

> Habakkuk 1.2, 13

Though he found no easy answer, he continued to believe in God's sovereignty over men and nations, saying, "If it seems slow, wait for it; it will surely come." In the meantime, "the righteous shall live by his faith" (Hab 2.3-4).

Jehoiakim endured three years of submission to the new Babylonian conquerors before he rejected the advice of Jeremiah (Jer 27.9-11) and revolted. When he refused to send the customary tribute to Babylon, Nebuchadnezzar, by now the king, acted swiftly to crush the rebellion. He sent his army to invade Judah and he himself arrived to direct the siege of Jerusalem. Before the city fell in 597 B.C. Jehoiakim died or was murdered, perhaps by Judah's pro-Babylonian party whose members blamed the nation's disaster on the king's pro-Egyptian policy.

Punishment for the rebellion now fell on Jehoiakim's eighteen-year-old son Jehoiachin (Jeconiah) (2 Kings 24.6-15; 25.27-30; 2 Chron 36.8-10). He ruled only three months before being forced to surrender to the Babylonians. They exiled the king, his family, and three thousand leading citizens of Judah, including the prophet Ezekiel, sending them to Babylon. There Jehoiachin continued to live as a captive monarch for thirty-seven years.

Zedekiah (Mattaniah) (2 Kings 24.17-25.7; 2 Chron 36.10-21), Josiah's third son and an uncle of the exiled king, was appointed by Nebuchadnezzar to rule Judah as regent. During this eleven-year regency, the prophet Jeremiah advised Zedekiah to submit to Babylonian demands. "Bring your necks under the yoke of the king of Babylon, and serve him and his people, and live . . . . Why should this city become a desolation?" (Jer 27.12,17). Unwisely, Zedekiah disregarded the prophet's advice and, influenced by the war party of Judah and promises of help from Egypt, defied Babylonia.

Again Nebuchadnezzar reacted swiftly and with great brutality. For a second time he besieged Jerusalem, which held out against him during a year and a half of terrible suffering. Finally, in 587 B.C., Nebuchadnezzar stormed the city and, according to Babylonian records, entered it through a breach in the walls. He set the Temple on fire together with the palaces and all the great houses, demolished the city walls, and removed the Temple treasures to Babylon. When Zedekiah, the last king of the royal line of David, tried to escape from the doomed city, he was intercepted and taken prisoner. After witnessing the slaying of his sons, he was blinded and led away in fetters to Babylon.

The conquerors deported the prominent citizens of Jerusalem, who then joined the earlier captives of 597 B.C. in Babylon. Only the poorest people were left in Judah to eke out their existence in a ruined land. The suffering and desolation of Judah following the siege and capture of Jerusalem is conveyed in the solemn dirges of the Book of Lamentations.

How lonely sits the city
    that was full of people!
How like a widow has she become,
    she that was great among the nations!
She that was a princess among the cities
    has become a vassal.

Lamentations 1.1

With the conquest of Judah, the national life seemed doomed to extinction. In writing of this ancient crisis in his book, *My People,* Abba Eban, the Israeli statesman, says, "History seemed to have come full circle. The descendants of Abraham had left the shores of the Euphrates at the dawn of history. They now returned as prisoners and deportees."

Nebuchadnezzar appointed Gedaliah (2 Kings 25.22-25), a friend of the prophet Jeremiah and a wise and chivalrous official, to be governor of Judah. Because Jerusalem was in ruins, Gedaliah ruled from Mizpah, but after two months in power he was treacherously murdered by those who condemned his policy of submission to Babylonia. His supporters fled to Egypt and forced the aged Jeremiah to go with them (Jer 41.1-43.7). Judah now lost her identity as a nation and became merely one of the administrative units of the Babylonian Empire. Most of her people had been dispersed and were living as exiles in Babylonia and Egypt.

Part Five
Exile, Rebirth, and Foreign Domination

Chapter 21 **The Babylonian Exile**

587-538 B.C.

Paradoxically, the catastrophe that destroyed Judah and exiled thousands of her citizens not only failed to obliterate the people of the covenant, the people of Israel, but it brought about a renewal of their age-old faith. During the Exile, Judah itself remained a ruined and destitute land, stripped of its leaders, its cities destroyed, and its farms, orchards, and vineyards reverting to wilderness. Meanwhile, the exiles in Babylon were, on the whole, well treated by their conquerors. They lived together in several large communities whose affairs were directed by groups of elders (Ezek 8.1). The Judeans engaged in the busy commercial life of Babylonia and prospered. At various periods some of them even rose to be important officials at the Babylonian, and later at the Persian, court, as the stories about Zerubbabel, Nehemiah, and Daniel indicate. Most important of all, the spiritual life of the people did not wither away in exile, but matured and deepened under the inspiration of many religious leaders, including such prophets as Jeremiah, Ezekiel, and the anonymous one whose poetic messages of hope are preserved in Isaiah 40-55 and who is therefore called Second Isaiah or the Babylonian Isaiah.

For decades the prophets had warned of coming disaster. Once the terrible blow fell, the Judeans perceived that the spiritual insight of their prophets had been true—that God's survival was not bound up with the fortunes of his people, but that he was the eternal Lord of the whole earth. All that had happened to them was not some inexplicable calamity, but the Lord's judgment upon his disobedient people. They now expected God, acting in mercy, to save "a remnant" of them and give them a new covenant.

As has already been noted, the great prophet Jeremiah explained the meaning of this new covenant. He implied that the institutional religion of the past, which had been centered in Jerusalem, was not enough, for he saw that henceforth God would write his laws in each man's heart and a man's response to the Lord would be inward and personal. Jeremiah's practical advice to the exiles of 597 B.C. emphasized that, despite exile, they were still the people of God:

> "Thus says the Lord of hosts, the God of Israel, to all the exiles whom I have sent to exile from Jerusalem to Babylon: Build houses and live in them; plant gardens and eat their produce. Take wives and have sons and daughters . . . multiply there, and do not decrease. But seek the welfare of the city where I have sent you into exile, and pray to the Lord on its behalf, for in its welfare you will find your welfare."
>
> Jeremiah 29.4-7

Ezekiel, like Jeremiah, saw his homeland of Judah die, crushed by the might of Babylonia. Nevertheless, because both prophets believed so intensely that the Lord reigned supreme over all the nations of the world and that the events of history were in his hands, they were confident that he would somehow cause his people to live again. Ezekiel had been among the first Judeans deported to

Babylonia in 597 B.C. When news of the fall of Jerusalem and the destruction of the Temple finally reached him, he had already been an exile in a foreign land for twelve years (Ezek 33.21). Throughout this time he had been sustained by a vision of "the glory of the Lord" sitting upon a sapphire throne and surrounded by ineffable radiance in which were wheels and fire and four living creatures each having the face of a man, a lion, an ox, or an eagle (Ezek 1.4-28). In the midst of this overpowering vision, he heard a voice,

> "Son of man, stand upon your feet, and I will speak with you . . . . I send you to the people of Israel, to a nation of rebels . . . . And you shall speak my words to them . . . ."
>
> Ezekiel 2.1, 3, 7

The words Ezekiel spoke inspired his countrymen to hope that, as with the dry bones in the valley he described, the Spirit of God would make them live again and restore them to their own land (Ezek 37.1-14). Besides hope, Ezekiel also gave the exiles a blueprint for their life in the future. Essentially, they were to be, as in their old tribal days, a worshiping community. They would live in the holy city of Jerusalem. Their life would be dominated by worship in the Temple, and by the Law as expounded by priests and Levites. "I . . . will set my sanctuary in the midst of them for evermore. My dwelling place shall be with them; and I will be their God and they shall be my people . . . ." (Ezek 37.26-27). With such messages, Ezekiel introduced into the faith of Israel a spirituality that redeemed the narrow priestly and ritual elements of his teachings.

Among Ezekiel's fellow captives were those who not only meditated upon the meaning of all that had befallen Judah but also studied the scrolls of their sacred writings brought with them to Babylonia. In the light of their recent history, they began to revise and edit and combine the ancient historical documents, thus preparing the so-called priestly edition of the Pentateuch. Other writers, known as the Deuteronomic historians because they had been influenced by the Book of Deuteronomy, began to rewrite and record the entire sweep of Israel's history to about 550 B.C. Thus the Bible as a literary entity, a collection of sacred books, began to take the form in which we have it today.

Now that the destroyed Temple could no longer be a rallying center, the Sabbath became the link binding together all the descendants of the Judeans living in foreign lands. On the Sabbath they gathered to pray and to read the sacred writings, thus laying the foundations of synagogue worship. In this period of political death and spiritual rebirth, they enjoyed one of their most creative periods. While the faith of Israel emerged as a religion that transcends a particular place and offers a universal message, the people themselves maintained their identity as a special community—the people of God.

Chapter 22 **Judea Under the Persians**
538-332 B.C.

Not long after the death of Nebuchadnezzar, his Babylonian empire fell to the Persian conqueror Cyrus the Great. Cyrus had already upset the balance of power in the region by annexing Media, defeating King Croesus of Lydia, and gaining control of Asia Minor. In 539 B.C., after the gates of Babylon were opened to him, Cyrus established in that city one of the centers of his extensive empire, which for two centuries dominated the ancient world.

About 540 B.C., shortly before Cyrus took Babylon, a new prophet, Second Isaiah, brought a vibrant message of hope to his discouraged fellow exiles. By now many of them were wearied of captivity and lamented,

By the waters of Babylon, there we sat down and wept,
    when we remembered Zion.
On the willows there
    we hung up our lyres.
• • • • • • • • • • • • •
How shall we sing the Lord's song
    in a foreign land?

Psalm 137.1-2, 4

Second Isaiah's prophecies begin with a mighty burst of hope and comfort in a transcendent chapter that summarizes his message.

> Comfort, comfort my people
> > says your God.
> Speak tenderly to Jerusalem,
> > and cry to her
> that her warfare is ended,
> > that her iniquity is pardoned.
>
> • • • • • • • • • • • • •
>
> And the glory of the Lord shall be revealed,
> > and all flesh shall see it together.
>
> > > > Isaiah 40.1-2, 5

Second Isaiah mentions Cyrus by name as the agent of God sent to restore the people of Israel (Isa 44.28-45.4). In a world-embracing vision, he speaks for the Lord who is no longer regarded as the exclusive deity of Israel, but as the Savior of the whole earth.

> "Turn to me and be saved,
> > all the ends of the earth!
> > For I am God, and there is no other."
>
> > > > Isaiah 45.22

One of Cyrus' first acts upon coming to power in Babylon was to issue an edict (Ezra 1.2-4; 6.3-5) that authorized the exiled Jews to return to their country. This was an instance of the liberal Persian policy of allowing subject peoples to live in their own land according to their own customs and religion—a policy in stark contrast to the "scorched earth" practices of the Assyrians and Babylonians, who had destroyed cities and temples, emptied treasuries, and dispersed whole populations.

The first group of exiles that returned to Jerusalem were led by Sheshbazzar, who was apparently a son of the exiled king Jehoiachin and thus a ruler with a claim to legitimacy. The settlers, though fired with religious zeal, found their country in such a ruined condition that their first concern was to build homes and raise enough crops to sustain themselves. They did, however, lay the foundations for a new place of worship in Jerusalem. Work on this lagged until they were spurred on by the prophets Haggai and Zechariah and by the Persian-appointed governor, Zerubbabel, nephew and successor of Sheshbazzar. Finally, in 515 B.C., they completed a smaller and less imposing Temple than the one Solomon had built and the Babylonians had destroyed.

Disturbances within the Persian Empire on the accession to the throne of Darius the Great in 522 B.C. awakened a dream among the returned exiles of restoring the kingdom of David. This dream centered on Zerubbabel who, as a grandson of Jehoiachin, the exiled king of Judah, and thus a prince of the royal line of David, was believed by many to be the promised messiah (Hag. 2.21-23). But the Persians, possibly on learning of this, may have recalled Zerubbabel from Jerusalem, for the Bible is silent about his later life. All hopes for the restoration of an independent state ended at this time. Judah, which after the exile was called Judea (Ezra 9.9), became, with Syria, Phoenicia, and the rest of Palestine, one of the twenty provinces, or satrapies, of the Persian Empire. Within its own satrapy, called by its Persian administrators "Beyond the River" (Ezra 4.10), Judea began to emerge as a small, semi-independent commonwealth ruled by priests.

Judea remained poor and sparsely settled for many years because the greater number of exiled Judeans, or Jews as they were now known (Neh 1.2), chose to remain in Babylonia or Egypt. Here they established strong and enduring communities, the one in Babylonia remaining pre-eminent until about A.D. 1000. These and Jewish communities in other countries became known as the Diaspora, or the Jews of the Dispersion (Jn 7.35).

One of these Jewish settlements was founded, between

570 and 525 B.C., on the river-island of Elephantine in the Nile near Aswan in Upper Egypt. Here a market for ivory tusks and a military outpost had been established. The Elephantine Papyri, which came to light in A.D. 1893, consist of legal texts and letters written by the Jews who settled here in the time of Ezra. They mention a temple of Yahweh in which the colonists performed religious ceremonies similar to those of Jerusalem.

Nearly a hundred years after the first exiles returned to Jerusalem, the Jews in and around the city lived without adequate protection because the Persians had forbidden them to rebuild the city walls. As a result, neighboring Arabs, Edomites, Ammonites, and even their kindred Samaritans constantly harassed or attacked them. Learning of the desperate plight of his countrymen, Nehemiah, a young Jewish official at the court of Artaxerxes I in Susa, requested the king to appoint him Persian governor of Judea. In 445 B.C. he obtained a commission to rebuild the ruined walls of Jerusalem. After completing this task, he returned for a second governorship and strengthened the city's social and political life, thus re-establishing Jerusalem as the national and religious center of Judea. Due primarily to his foresight and energy, the people of Israel recovered their identity, though not their independence.

It is not entirely clear whether Ezra the scribe, with a group of two thousand exiles, returned to Jerusalem before Nehemiah's governorship or after it. Ezra's mission as both priest and scribe was to revive and regulate the religious life of the people. He called together "into the square before the Water Gate" of Jerusalem a great assembly of men, women, and children. Standing on a wooden pulpit made for the purpose, with the important men of the community on his right and on his left, Ezra read from "the book of the law" from early morning until midday. This book, which Ezra had brought from Babylonia, was probably the revised and rewritten Pentateuch completed by the priests during the Exile. The Pentateuch was written in Hebrew, but by this time many of the Jewish people spoke a closely related language, Aramaic, which was the international language of the region and the one used in the various states of the Persian Empire. Therefore, when the Pentateuch was read to the people it had to be explained or translated for them. Accordingly, when Ezra finished the reading of the Law, or possibly only excerpts from it, the Levites "gave the sense, so that the people understood the reading" (Neh 8.8). This was one of the functions of the Levites: to interpret the Law when it was read in the public assemblies and to explain the meaning of Israel's faith.

During the next seven days, which were celebrated as the Feast of Tabernacles (Sukkoth), the people lived in booths made of cut branches, and Ezra continued the reading of the Law (Neh 8.13-18). Finally, in a solemn climax, the people confessed their sins, Ezra offered a long prayer for them, the covenant itself was signed, and everyone took an oath "to walk in God's law which was given by Moses . . . and to observe and do all the commandments of the Lord. . . ." (Neh 10.29).

Ezra taught that Israel had a unique destiny as a holy nation, and he believed that racial purity must be preserved in order to fulfill that destiny. The theme of fidelity to the Law dominated this teaching, and he made the Law the basis of Israel's life.

Israel, under Ezra, regained her sense of being the special people of God and achieved a new unity that was never lost. From this time on, the Scriptures dominated Jewish life, and the Jews became a religious community ruled both politically and religiously by priestly families. Because of her remote position far from the mainstream of history, and her weak impoverished condition, Judea, the Jewish state after the Exile, inevitably turned inward, thus deepening and developing her spiritual life.

The two hundred years of the Persian period was an era of literary activity among the Jews. In the light of Ezra's reforms, an unknown chronicler (perhaps Ezra himself) rewrote Israel's history in order to highlight the importance of the Temple and the priesthood. He used earlier histories and personal journals, combining and editing them to produce the books of 1 and 2 Chronicles, Ezra, and Nehemiah.

Among the prophets of this period, in addition to Second Isaiah, were five or more others, including Haggai and Zechariah, who have already been mentioned as urging the building of the second Temple in Jerusalem. Malachi spoke for sincerity in worship, the sanctity of the priesthood, and the sanctity of marriage. Obadiah's denunciation of Judah's old enemy, Edom, contains this prophet's conviction that godless men cannot forever refuse to heed the righteousness of God. Joel in the midst of a plague of locusts called the people of Israel to repentance.

Three stories written probably in this period, namely, Ruth, Jonah, and Esther, reveal some of the crosscurrents of thought popular at this time. Ruth suggests that harsh laws enforcing racial purity, like those of the time of Nehemiah and Ezra, were not in the best interests of the nation, for was not Ruth, the Moabitess, the great grandmother of King David? Jonah is not entirely a story of a great fish, but a protest against bigotry and a message of God's love for all peoples. Esther is nationalistic rather than religious in tone and reflects the popularity of the Feast of Purim with which it was associated.

Three books of Israel's wisdom literature, namely, Job, Proverbs, and Ecclesiastes, as well as some of her poetry, including the Song of Solomon and the Psalms, may all have been written or expanded during the literary flowering of the Persian period.

Chapter 23 **The Greek Period**
332-167 B.C.

The conquests of Alexander the Great are not recorded in the Old Testament because its historical accounts end with Nehemiah and Ezra in the Persian period. The impact of Alexander's victories, however, is obliquely noted in Daniel where, after a reference to the Babylonian, Median, and Persian empires, Alexander's vast empire is characterized as "a fourth kingdom, strong as iron . . . which shall break and crush" the previous kingdoms (Dan 2.40). In other visions, this Greek empire is seen as a dragon-like beast (Dan 7.7) and a he-goat (Dan 8.5).

Politically, Alexander's conquest of Palestine made little difference to the Jews because he adopted the Persian policy of allowing subject provinces to govern themselves locally. The real impact of Alexander's conquests was religious and cultural. Alexander, having been a pupil of the Greek philosopher Aristotle, was bent on spreading Greek culture. Thus, in the wake of his armies, Greek ideals and ways of life began to penetrate the Middle East, transforming many areas of Palestine into centers of a Greek-like culture called Hellenism. This caused profound changes in Hebrew thought. A few of the books of the Bible, including Ecclesiastes, Daniel, and some of the psalms and proverbs reflect the influence of Greek ideas. The Jews watched, some with approving interest, others with apprehension, while theaters, temples, gymnasiums, and statues—all foreign to Hebrew culture and habits—were erected in thirty new Greek cities established in the region. Wealthy, aristocratic Jews, finding that Hellenism introduced them to a free world of thought beyond the rigid framework of Judaism, welcomed the changes introduced by the Greeks. Other, more pious Jews feared Alexander's dream of "one world" and perceived that the Greek ideal of uniting mankind in a single family, bound together by a common culture, conflicted with the idea of Jewish uniqueness under the Law of Moses. Pious Jews, therefore, opposed Hellenism and resolutely defended the faith of their fathers in the Lord God of Israel and his Law.

This basic conflict between Judaism and Hellenism (a conflict of ideals finally resolved in Christianity) was fought inconclusively during the Greek and early Roman periods. By introducing Hellenism, Alexander's conquests ended Judea's isolation and brought her people into the mainstream of history. Thus the world into which Christianity came was enriched by two of the highest cultural developments of antiquity. Christianity became the heir not only of Jewish monotheism and its rich spiritual history, but also of Greek culture, philosophy, and the ideal of world brotherhood.

Outside of Palestine many aspects of Greek culture were eagerly adopted by the Jews. In Egypt in 332 B.C., Alexander founded a new port at the mouth of the Nile and named the city for himself. He welcomed Jews to Alexandria, giving them citizenship and complete religious freedom. As a result, so many Jews were attracted to this Greek commercial and intellectual city that Alexandria became, next to Jerusalem, the chief center of Jewish life. One rabbi declared that not to have seen Alexandria's central synagogue, an imposing basilica adorned with a double row of columns, was never to have seen the glory achieved by Israel.

Beginning in the 3rd century B.C., a Greek translation of the Scriptures was made for the Greek-speaking Jews of Alexandria, who could no longer understand Hebrew. It was called the Septuagint, meaning "of seventy," in reference to its legendary seventy translators who were said to have translated independently, but whose seventy renderings were all found to be identical.

After the break-up of Alexander's empire at his death in 323 B.C., his two Greek generals, Seleucus and Ptolemy, divided the Middle East between themselves, Seleucus taking Syria, and Ptolemy, Egypt. Because both claimed Palestine, it changed hands between them five times in twenty-two years. In 301 B.C. the Ptolemaic dynasty of Egypt succeeded in taking over the disputed country from the Seleucid empire of Syria and in dominating it for a hundred or so years. The Ptolemaic kings continued the policy of granting the Jews local self-government. During this period they were ruled by their Council of Elders, called the Sanhedrin, under the leadership of the high priest.

Syria finally annexed Palestine in 198 B.C., when Antiochus III of Syria defeated the forces of the infant king Ptolemy V near the source of the Jordan at Paneas and occupied Jerusalem. The Jews welcomed this change of rulers and the Sanhedrin sent a delegation to greet the Syrian king when he entered their city. Though he granted his new subjects religious freedom and many privileges, these were taken from them in 175 B.C. on the accession of his son Antiochus IV, who was called Epiphanes because he claimed to be Zeus manifest (*theos epiphanes*).

If the new Syrian king thought that the Jews would meekly adopt the worship of pagan gods and the Hellenistic customs he forced upon them, he was greatly mistaken. To further his policy of destroying Judaism and promoting Hellenism, he forbade the Jews to observe the Sabbath, to make the sacrifices required by the Law, to practice circumcision, or to possess the books of Scripture. Moreover, every Jew was required to make sacrifices to the Greek gods. Disobedience of this requirement was punishable as treason to the state. In 168 B.C. Antiochus marched his soldiers into the Temple itself and, upon the very altar of burnt offering, erected a pagan statue to Zeus. Here swine, an "unclean" animal according to Jewish law, were sacrificed. The Jews regarded this as "the abomination that makes desolate" (Dan 11.31).

Some of the Hellenistic Jews applauded Antiochus' policy, but the mass of the people resisted this first recorded religious persecution of their history. According to 1 Maccabees in the Apocrypha, "many in Israel stood firm . . . . They chose to die rather than to be defiled by [unclean] food or to profane the holy covenant; and they did die. And very great wrath came upon Israel" (1 Macc 1.62-63).

In the midst of this terror, the unknown author of the Book of Daniel wrote to inspire courage in his fellow Jews and to renew their faith that the Lord who directs the affairs of nations would, in the end, establish his kingdom. Because this author could not write openly of the political situation, he concealed his message in a new form of prophecy called an apocalypse, a word derived from the Greek *apocalypto*, meaning "reveal, disclose." Apocalypses, which had already appeared in such books of prophecy as Isaiah, Ezekiel, and Zechariah, were supposed to reveal the consummation of history, when God would intervene to save his people. Daniel, in common with other writers of apocalypses, used the elaborate imagery of numbers, signs, symbols, visions, and stories from the past to announce and, at the same time, to veil his revelations. To the Syrian authorities, Daniel's revelations must have seemed weird and unintelligible, but to Jewish readers who knew how to interpret an apocalypse Daniel's message brought new hope and courage and must have been a factor in the success of the Maccabean uprising.

Part Six
Independence and the Hasmonean Period

Chapter 24 The Maccabean Revolt
167-142 B.C.

1 Maccabees 1-16; 2 Maccabees 8-15

The religious persecution of Antiochus IV Epiphanes touched off a bitter revolt of the Jews against the imperialism and culture of the Hellenistic world. In the little mountain village of Modein northwest of Jerusalem, the old priest Mattathias, of the priestly family of Hashmon, refused to sacrifice to heathen gods. "Even if all the nations that live under the rule of the king obey him," Mattathias declared, "yet I and my sons and my brothers will live by the covenant of our fathers. Far be it from us to desert the law and the ordinances . . . ." (1 Macc 2.19-20). In defense of his faith he killed the officer sent to enforce the royal decrees and raised the cry of rebellion, "Let everyone who is zealous for the law and supports the covenant come out with me!" (1 Macc 2.27).

Immediately Mattathias with his five sons and their followers fled to the Judean wilderness where the militant religious sect of the Hasidim joined them (1 Macc 2.42). The revolutionaries soon gathered a guerrilla band, which, after successfully attacking the Syrians, won wide support among the Jews.

Judas, called Maccabeus, meaning "The Hammer" (1 Macc 3.1-9.22), became leader of the revolt after the death of his father, Mattathias. He proved to be an inspiring leader and an exceptionally brilliant general with immense personal courage. Before battle he used to pray (1 Macc 4.30) and he rallied his men with the cry, "It is better for us to die in battle than to see the misfortunes of our nation and of the sanctuary. But as his will in heaven may be, so he will do" (1 Macc 3.59-60). In 164 B.C., after successful campaigns against the Syrian forces, Judas freed the Temple in Jerusalem from foreign control, purified it of defilement, and rededicated the altar to the worship of Yahweh. For the ceremony beginning on the twenty-fifth of Kislev at the time of the winter solstice, only enough oil was found to keep the lamp burning for one day. Miraculously, however, the oil lasted through the eight days of the festival, an event celebrated in the Feast of Lights, or the Feast of Dedication (Jn. 10.22), and remembered today in the Jewish festival of Hanukkah, meaning, "dedication."

Realizing that the Jewish patriots had indeed defeated him, Antiochus withdrew his religious decrees and suspended his persecution of the Jews. The Hasidim, satisfied with this achievement of religious freedom, planned to withdraw from the struggle, but Judas Maccabeus, who had by now tasted military success and whose piety and patriotism were blended, fought on for political independence from the Syrians. After many military exploits he died a hero's death in 160 B.C., having inspired in his countrymen a patriotism that demanded courage and active service.

Jonathan, the brother of Judas, led the fight for freedom from 160 to 142 B.C., when he was treacherously murdered at Ptolemais (Acre) (1 Macc 9.23-12.53). He was the fourth son of Mattathias to die violently. John had been killed in an early phase of the war. Eleazar was crushed to death in an attack by Syrian elephants (1 Macc 6.30, 43-46).

Chapter 25 Priest-Kings of the Hasmonean Dynasty

142-63 B.C.

At Jonathan's death the leadership of the Jews passed to Simon (142-134 B.C.), the last surviving son of Mattathias (1 Macc 13-16). Exercising his gift for statesmanship, Simon negotiated a treaty with the Syrians that recognized Jewish independence. "The yoke of the Gentiles was removed from Israel" (1 Macc 13.41), exulted the historian of this period. For the first time since the reign of Josiah in the 7th century, the Jews were free from political domination. In gratitude to Simon, the people made him their commander and governor, and bestowed upon him and his descendants the right to rule as hereditary high priests. As a sign of his new princely rank, the Jews decided that Simon should be "clothed in purple and wear gold" (1 Macc 14.43). Thus the Hasmonean dynasty was established, a dynasty that derived its name from Hashmon, an ancestor, or perhaps the father, of Mattathias.

Simon organized his government and consolidated the territories he and his brothers had won. At the height of his ascendancy he and two of his sons were invited to a banquet at Jericho given by his ambitious and scheming son-in-law. At the banquet not only was Simon assassinated, but also two of his sons were captured and later murdered. Simon was the fifth and last of the sons of Mattathias to die violently.

The third son of the murdered Simon outwitted the assassination plot and as John Hyrcanus I (134-104 B.C.) soon had himself installed as high priest and prince of

Judea by the Jews. With the accession to power of the third generation of Hasmoneans their patriotism became secondary to their ambition and worldliness. John Hyrcanus seized the opportunity of waning Syrian power to embark on conquest in an attempt to restore to the Jews the entire kingdom once ruled by David. He subdued Idumea, lying south of Judea, as well as lower Galilee and Samaria, thus making his kingdom the dominant military power of the region. In an unwise move he destroyed the Samaritan temple on Mount Gerizim, thus deepening the enmity between Samaritans and Jews. This later produced a situation in which, according to the Samaritan women whom Jesus met at the well, "Jews have no dealings with Samaritans" (Jn 4.9). In violation of the Jewish ideal of religious freedom, John Hyrcanus forced Judaism on the states he had defeated, an action that alienated the Pharisees who had been his supporters. Later they would interpret the accession of the hated and feared Idumean prince Herod to the throne of Judea as punishment for the religious oppression of Idumea by John Hyrcanus.

His reign was partly responsible for the rise of religious parties and the bitter rivalry that grew up between them. John Hyrcanus transferred his support from the Pharisees to the Sadducees, a small, powerful group representing the wealthy families, the Hellenists, and the priestly hierarchy. The name *Sadducee* was probably derived from Zadok, the high priest who had anointed Solomon (1 Kings 1.38-39). The Sadducees were men of the world, shrewder and more politically motivated than devout. They formed the conservative party with a vested interest in the Temple treasury, the rituals, and the sacrifices of the Temple. Their control of the Sanhedrin, which served as the council of the Hasmonean rulers, gave them great power.

The Pharisees were members of a movement drawn from all sections of the people, including laymen, scribes, priests, and even some members of the high priestly families. They formed the majority party and their study, worship, and deeds of charity were centered in the synagogue. Firmly opposed to the political imperialism of the Hasmonean dynasty, the Pharisees hoped to create a better society by bringing every aspect of life into obedience to the Law to which they were deeply devoted. Unlike the Sadducees, however, they did not blindly follow the letter of the written Law, but acknowledged the validity of the Oral Torah. They tried to discover the underlying spirit of the Law and apply it to the conditions of their time. In this they were like Jesus (Mt 5.21-22). The Gospels report instances of Pharisees who eagerly listened to him and even supported him. On the other hand, many of the more narrow-minded Pharisees, whose chief concern was to protect Israel's great ideals from being submerged in a rising tide of Hellenism, opposed Jesus because they feared that his teachings and actions were contrary to their holy Law.

To protest the increasing worldliness of John Hyrcanus and his failure to uphold the aims of the Maccabean revolt, a new religious group appeared. This was the sect of the Essenes. They despaired of reforming either the state or organized religion and some of them retired to remote areas where they formed communities dedicated to holiness. Here they lived ascetic lives, studied the Scriptures, and awaited the coming of a messiah to establish a spiritual kingdom. The Essene movement illustrates the spiritual ferment of the period that preceded the ministry of Jesus. The sect that produced the Dead Sea Scrolls in its monastery at Qumran is thought by many to have been related to the Essenes if not itself an Essene community.

With John Hyrcanus, the Hasmoneans ceased to be truly national leaders, and therefore opposition to them increased among the Jews. The Greek customs adopted by the Hasmoneans, their use of foreign mercenaries to keep their own subjects under control, their desire for conquest, their great brutality, and their disregard of the Law, extinguished the people's respect for a dynasty of princely high-priests who were descended neither from the royal line of David nor from the priestly house of Aaron.

Two sons of John Hyrcanus succeeded their father. The elder one, Aristobulus I (Judas) (104-103 B.C.), continued his father's conquests. He may have been the king who put to death the "Teacher of Righteousness," leader of a pious sect of the Essenes that later moved to Qumran near the Dead Sea. Aristobolus I subjugated upper Galilee and imposed Jewish beliefs and customs upon the region that became the scene of Jesus' early ministry.

His brother, Alexander Janneus (Jonathan) (103-76 B.C.), waged almost constant war and, in his appetite for conquest, extended the boundaries of the Hasmonean kingdom to its greatest extent. At home he incurred the bitter hatred of the Pharisees because of his cruelty in crushing their rebellion. He was the first Hasmonean to use on his coinage the title "king." He minted bronze coins with the Hebrew legend, "Jonathan the King," on the obverse, and the Greek legend, "King Alexander," on the reverse.

The next ruler was a woman, Alexandra Salome (76-67 B.C.). She had been married to Aristobulus I, but, at his death, in accordance with the levirate law (Deut 25.5), she became the wife of his brother Alexander Janneus. He bequeathed his throne to Alexandra Salome and his high priesthood to his elder son, Hyrcanus, a quiet, unambitious man. The younger, more dynamic son, Aristobulus, was excluded from high office, largely, no doubt, because he opposed his mother's policy of conciliating the Pharisees. Salome proved to be an able ruler who wisely invited the Pharisees into her council and accepted their advice. After giving the country its only nine years of peace and prosperity in the eighty years of Hasmonean rule, she died at the age of seventy-three.

Civil strife broke out after the queen's death, bringing an end to Jewish independence and eventually causing the downfall of the Hasmonean dynasty. Aristobulus II (67-63 B.C.) quickly seized the high priesthood and the royal crown, both of which rightfully belonged to his older brother Hyrcanus. Left to himself Hyrcanus would undoubtedly have returned to private life, and civil war between the two sons of Alexandra Salome would have been avoided. But Antipater, the ambitious governor of Idumea and father of Herod the Great, seeking his own advantage in the troubled situation, persuaded Hyrcanus to oppose his brother's usurpation. After a bitter struggle, the royal brothers separately appealed their quarrel to the Roman general Pompey, who by then had conquered much of the Middle East. Aristobulus II rashly prepared to attack the Romans. Thereupon, Pompey imprisoned the Jewish king; seized Jerusalem in 63 B.C.; desecrated the Temple by entering the Holy of Holies; massacred twelve thousand Jews; sent many others to the Roman slave market; and paraded Aristobulus, accompanied by his two sons Alexander and Antigonus, through the streets of Rome as a captive king. The Jewish community now became subject to Roman rule and the freedom won with so much sacrifice by the first Hasmoneans disappeared.

Table 1

The Hasmonean Dynasty

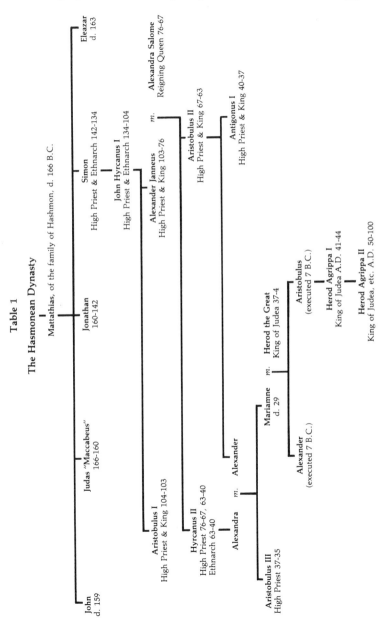

Mattathias, of the family of Hashmon. d. 166 B.C.

John
d. 159

Judas "Maccabeus"
166-160

Jonathan
160-142

Simon
High Priest & Ethnarch 142-134

Eleazar
d. 163

John Hyrcanus I
High Priest & Ethnarch 134-104

Aristobulus I
High Priest & King 104-103

Alexander Janneus
High Priest & King 103-76

Alexandra Salome
Reigning Queen 76-67

Hyrcanus II
High Priest 76-67, 63-40
Ethnarch 63-40

Aristobulus II
High Priest & King 67-63

Alexandra   *m.*

Antigonus I
High Priest & King 40-37

Aristobulus III
High Priest 37-35

Alexander

Alexandra   *m.*

Alexander
(executed 7 B.C.)

Mariamne
d. 29

m.   Herod the Great
King of Judea 37-4

Aristobulus
(executed 7 B.C.)

Herod Agrippa I
King of Judea A.D. 41-44

Herod Agrippa II
King of Judea, etc. A.D. 50-100

Part Seven
Under Roman Rule

Chapter 26 **The Last Hasmonean Rulers**

63-37 B.C.

The Romans reinstated Hyrcanus II (63-40 B.C.) in the high priesthood, the office he had held in his mother's reign, because they saw that he was the more amenable of the two Hasmonean brothers. They deprived him, however, of his title of king, demoting him to the status of *ethnarch*, "ruler of a people." Hyrcanus II now presided over a truncated and separated realm consisting only of Judea, Perea, Galilee, and Idumea, all other parts of the once extensive Hasmonean empire, including the Decapolis, Samaria, Jezreel, and the Mediterranean coastal cities, being under the Roman governor of Syria. The ineffective Hyrcanus II ruled in name only, for Antipater the Idumean, who was his astute chief minister, remained the power behind the throne. Antipater appointed his eldest son, Phasael, governor of Jerusalem and his second son, the able but ruthless Herod, governor of Galilee. When Antipater died from poisoning in 43 B.C., Herod occupied a strategic position in the Jewish state.

For a brief period, Antigonus I (40-37 B.C.), son of the deposed Aristobulus II, having managed to escape from Rome, joined forces with the Parthians whose empire, then at the height of its power, was menacing the Roman frontier in Syria. With the help of the Parthians, Antigonus seized and ruled the realm of his uncle Hyrcanus II, depriving him of his high priesthood and banishing him to the Jewish community in Babylon. Herod's brother Phasael was arrested and committed suicide in prison. Herod himself, fearing the intentions of the Parthians, placed his family in the lofty desert fortress of Masada near the Dead Sea, and fled to Rome on a ship provided by Cleopatra, queen of Egypt.

Mark Antony and Octavian (later known as Caesar Augustus, who was the first, and perhaps greatest, of the Roman Emperors) perceived that Herod had the ability and energy not only to control the turbulent Jews, but also to establish Judea as a bulwark for the Romans against Parthia and other eastern states. The Roman leaders, therefore, proposed that the senate revive the kingship of Judea and confer it upon Herod. As soon as the Roman Senate unanimously adopted the proposal, the new king of the Jews, walking between Antony and Octavian, went to deposit the decree in the Capitol and offer a sacrifice in the great temple of Jupiter Capitolinus.

King Herod wasted no time in returning to Judea where, with the help of the Romans, he set out to win his kingdom by force of arms. He eventually established his rule over Galilee, the lands of the Samaritans, Joppa, Gaza, and the unruly states east and northeast of Galilee. To give his reign the appearance of legitimacy he married the beautiful Hasmonean princess Mariamne, who, as granddaughter of Aristobulus II through her father and of Hyrcanus II through her mother, represented the two hostile branches of the Hasmonean dynasty. Herod captured Jerusalem in 37 B.C. and, according to his enemies, requested the Romans to execute Antigonus. It has been said that Antigonus was the first captive king ever beheaded by the Romans.

The death of Antigonus brought an end to a dynasty

that in eighty years had established an empire and compelled even Rome to acknowledge the importance and power of the Jewish state. Despite the terrible wars and civil disorders for which they were responsible, the Hasmoneans undoubtedly preserved the Jewish state from disintegrating during this chaotic period in the Middle East.

In saving the nation they also preserved Judaism. Though they themselves adopted the worst features of Hellenism and became worldly and ungodly, their era was one in which Judaism not only survived but grew strong. The Temple and its sacrifices were maintained. The Law was read, studied, and devotedly practiced. The Book of Psalms was completed. The Scriptures were collected and edited. During this period preceding the rise of Christianity the people's religious hopes and deep spiritual piety found expression in such groups as the Scribes, the Pharisees, the Essenes, and even in such nameless associations as that of the friends of the aged prophetess Anna "who were looking for the redemption of Jerusalem" (Lk 2.38).

The Hasmoneans, in presiding over this period of spiritual ferment and tragic strife, failed to resolve the basic conflict between Judaism and Hellenism, the conflict that had brought them into power in the first place. Their failure and that of Herod the Great made the Jewish disasters of A.D. 70 and 135 inevitable.

Chapter 27 Herod's Dynasty and the Beginning of the Christian Era
37 B.C.-A.D. 100

Herod the Great (37-4 B.C.), though king of the Jews, was only nominally Jewish. His mother, Cypros, was an Arabian princess from the powerful Nabataean kingdom; his father, Antipater, as noted above, an Idumean whose country had been forcibly converted to Judaism by John Hyrcanus I in the previous century. By cultural preference Herod was Greek, but by allegiance, Roman. He based his policy on cooperation with Rome, realizing that, if the Jewish people were to survive at all in a world dominated by Rome, they must abandon their separateness, adjust themselves to the outside world, and live peaceably within the Roman Empire. Many Jews opposed this policy, thus intensifying the basic conflict between themselves and the world around them, a conflict that Herod, despite his undeniable successes as a ruler, failed to settle. As a result, the conflict grew and long after his death exploded in catastrophe for the Jewish state.

The most important event of his reign and the one that ironically makes him notable in world history was the birth of Jesus "in the days of Herod, king of Judea" (Lk 1.5). Modern scholarship places this event late in Herod's reign, sometime between 7 and 4 B.C. Thus the thirty-three years of Herod's kingship largely explain the character of the period in which Jesus lived.

Herod served his Roman masters well by maintaining a high degree of order in an unruly part of the empire and by providing a bulwark on their eastern frontier. With his

Table 2

The Dynasty of Herod the Great

A Partial Genealogy with Biblical References

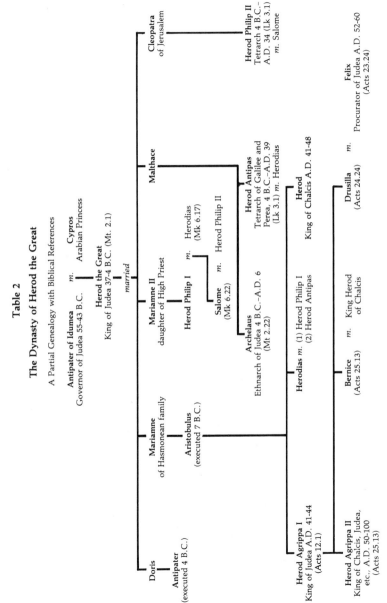

secret police he instituted a reign of terror that suppressed resistance to himself and to Rome. The peace he imposed and the public works he instituted brought full employment and great prosperity to Judea. He constructed a harbor at Caesarea and rebuilt the city of Samaria, renaming it Sebaste in honor of Augustus whose name in Greek was Sebastos. He also established a series of cities and fortresses in the Jordan valley; strengthened the fortress-palaces of Macherus and Masada on opposite shores of the Dead Sea; and built palaces and public buildings in Jericho, Jerusalem, and elsewhere, all in the Greco-Roman style that he admired.

To crown his life's work and win the good will of the Jews, Herod undertook an elaborate and magnificent reconstruction of the Temple of Jerusalem on a gigantic scale. The rabbis, however, said it was his "atonement for having slain so many sages of Israel." Begun in 20 B.C., the Temple was virtually complete in ten years, though building and repairs continued beyond the forty-six years mentioned in John 2.20, because the eastern retaining wall was not finished until A.D. 64. This was shortly before the entire Temple was utterly and finally destroyed by the Romans in A.D. 70.

Being of foreign origin, Herod could not combine the office of high priest with that of king, as had his Hasmonean predecessors, so he appointed to the holy office submissive men whom he frequently removed. He thus created a Sadducean aristocracy amenable to his policies.

The Jews as a whole, however, detested him for his disregard of the Law, his Hellenistic style of life, his despotism, and his ruthless cruelty. To them he seemed a monster. His fear and suspicion of the Hasmonean family, which he had driven from power, but into which he had married, never ceased. He murdered his wife Mariamne, her brother then serving as high priest, and her mother. Later, convinced that his two sons by Mariamne, Alexander and Aristobulus, were plotting against him, he had them executed. He also executed Antipater, his eldest son by his first wife Doris. During his last years, the palace intrigues and bitter rivalries of his quarreling family of ten wives, their relatives, and his ambitious children made him suspicious to the point of madness. The Gospel story of the massacre of the innocents (Mt 2.1-18) typifies one aspect of Herod's reign. As a whole it has been summarized by the scholar and former archbishop of Quebec, Philip Carrington, as, "a mixture of splendor and horror."

Herod's will divided his kingdom among three of his surviving sons: Archelaus, Herod Antipas, and Herod Philip, none of whom received the title of king from the Roman emperor Augustus. Archelaus (4 B.C.-A.D. 6) "reigned over Judea [also Samaria and Idumea] in place of his father Herod" (Mt 2.22) with the title of ethnarch. Inheriting all of his father's evil habits but none of his ability as a ruler, Archelaus outraged the Jews, and, after ten years of misrule, was deposed by the emperor and banished to Gaul. His realm was then incorporated into the Roman empire as a province administered by Roman prefects and later procurators. Their official residence was Caesarea, not Jerusalem. The prefect of Judea during the ministry of Jesus was Pontius Pilate (A.D. 26-36) (Lk 3.1), the Roman official who sentenced Jesus to death (Mk 15.1-15).

Judea now paid tribute directly to heathen Rome. Pious Jews, believing that tribute should be paid only to God, joined a group of fighters for freedom in a revolt led by "Judas the Galilean" (Acts 5.37). Though the Romans soon quelled this uprising, its spirit lived on in the new patriotic party of Zealots who advocated armed revolt against Rome.

Herod's second son, Herod Antipas, whom Jesus characterized as "that fox" (Lk 13.32), became the subordinate ruler, or tetrarch, of Galilee and Perea (4 B.C.–A.D. 39). He administered these provinces during the lifetime of John the Baptist and of Jesus. He imprisoned John the Baptist as a suspected revolutionary and later beheaded him at the request of his wife Herodias. She hated John because he had denounced her second marriage as unlawful, due to the fact that her first husband was a half-brother of her second husband (Mk 6.17-28). According to Luke's Gospel (23.6-12), Herod Antipas, visiting Jerusalem at the time of Jesus' arrest, received the controversial Galilean prisoner for questioning. When Jesus remained silent to his queries, Antipas astutely refused to become involved in Pilate's problem. After forty years of controlling the Galileans, Antipas, at his wife's urging, asked the Roman emperor for the title of king, but Caligula punished him for making this request by deposing and banishing him.

Herod Philip (4 B.C.–A.D. 34), "tetrarch of the region of Ituraea and Trachonitis" (Lk 3.1), was probably the best ruler among Herod the Great's three sons, for he attended personally to the administration of justice and adopted moderate policies. In the north of his non-Jewish tetrarchy, Philip rebuilt his capital of Paneas, renaming it Caesarea Philippi for Tiberius Caesar and himself. Jesus visited Caesarea Philippi with his disciples (Mk 8.27-30). Philip married Salome, daughter of Herodias and his half-brother, Herod Philip of Rome.

For a brief period, Judea, Galilee, and Perea were unified by the Romans under Herod Agrippa I (A.D. 41-44), a grandson of Herod the Great and also an heir of the Hasmoneans through his grandmother Mariamne, Herod's wife. With his sister Herodias, he had been educated in Rome and knew how to deal with imperial authorities and to please the emperors Caligula and Claudius. Herod Agrippa I is the king who executed the apostle James, the son of Zebedee, and imprisoned Peter (Acts 12.1-4). At his own sudden death he was survived by three daughters, Mariamne, Bernice, and Drusilla, and a seventeen-year-old son, Agrippa. As Agrippa was too young to reign, the Emperor Claudius reorganized the kingdom, making it a Roman province ruled by a procurator appointed by Rome.

Two of these procurators figure in the account of Paul's life. M. Antonius Felix (A.D. 52-60) married in succession three royal princesses, one of whom was Agrippa I's daughter, Drusilla. At Caesarea he heard Paul's case and listened to the apostle "speak upon faith in Christ Jesus" (Acts 24.1-26). Felix, who had made himself particularly hated by the Jews, was succeeded by an honest and able procurator, Porcius Festus (A.D. 60-62). He learned of Paul's case and sent Paul to Rome in response to the apostle's request (Acts 24.27-27.1).

When the son of Herod Agrippa I came of age, the Romans made him king of Chalcis, a small principality in the Lebanon mountains; later he became king of portions of the Roman province of Judea. As Herod Agrippa II (A.D. 53-100), he was the last ruler of the Herodian dynasty. Like his great-grandfather, Herod the Great, he was more like a Roman than a Jew, and, during a period of increasing hostility between Jews and Romans, he supported Rome. With his sister Bernice, later the mistress of the Emperor Titus, Agrippa listened to Paul defend his faith at Caesarea and discussed the matter with Festus, saying, "This man could have been set free if he had not appealed to Caesar" (Acts 26.32). Though Herod Agrippa II was not a practicing Jew, Paul politely characterized him as "especially familiar with all customs and controversies of the Jews" (Acts 26.3).

Chapter 28 The War Against the Romans
A.D. 66-73

Since the time of the Emperor Augustus, the Romans had guaranteed freedom of worship and other privileges to the Jews, but corrupt and cruel Roman prefects and procurators of Judea often failed to carry out official Roman policy. They were usually insensitive to Jewish religious scruples, imposed heavy taxation, largely to enrich themselves, and executed Jews at the first sign of revolt. When Pontius Pilate introduced into the very Temple itself banners portraying the Emperor Caligula, or when Felix had the high priest Jonathan murdered in the Temple precincts, Jewish enmity against the Romans flared up. Murder and brigandage became common in this tense situation and the country seethed in chaos.

Finally, the extremely nationalistic and militant party of the Zealots insisted that driving the Romans from Palestine was the only way to achieve peace and religious salvation. Another underground extremist group, a splinter party of the Zealots, was known as the Assassins, or Sicarii, from the short, curved daggers or *sicae* they wore. In Jerusalem, Paul was mistaken for the leader of the Assassins (Acts 21.38). Members of this fanatical group, disguising their violence as patriotism, terrorized the Jews as well as the Romans. It was rumored that Felix had hired them to murder the high priest Jonathan whose moderate policy they viewed as co-operation with Rome.

In this atmosphere of bitterness and anarchy, hatred of Rome finally flamed into open rebellion in A.D. 66. At the first news of the uprising, Nero, well aware of the power of his opponents, sent his most experienced general, Vespasian, with three legions and auxiliary troops, about sixty thousand men in all, to crush the rebels and restore order in Judea.

The events of this desperate struggle were recorded by an eyewitness, the Jewish historian, Josephus Flavius. At the outbreak of violence Josephus commanded the Jewish forces in Galilee. In A.D. 67, however, he defected to the winning side, adopted Vespasian's family name of Flavius, and served in the Roman army as an interpreter. Both his seven-volume *History of the Jewish War Against Rome*, published by order of Titus, and his twenty-volume *Jewish Antiquities* are prime sources for this period of Jewish history.

Vespasian subdued one rebellious district of Judea after another, but delayed attacking Jerusalem. There rival groups of terrorists were waging a civil war that seemed likely to end in the annihilation of all parties. At this time the Jewish Christians fled from the doomed city to Pella across the Jordan in the Decapolis. Vespasian, on being acclaimed emperor in A.D. 69, returned to Rome leaving his son Titus to end the war. Before Vespasian departed, the Romans destroyed the monastic center of the Dead Sea Sect at Qumran. Its members fled to nearby caves, taking their precious scrolls with them.

With eighty thousand men of four legions, Titus laid siege to Jerusalem, whose fortifications were manned by no more than twenty-five thousand Jewish soldiers. At the last moment, the rival Zealot factions still fighting among themselves within the city agreed to unite against Rome. Their truce, however, came too late. After starving the defenders and breaching the walls, Titus captured Jerusalem and killed many of its inhabitants in frightful massacres. The Romans entered the inner sanctuary of the Temple and burned it on the ninth of the Hebrew month of Ab (about August 28th), the anniversary of the Temple's destruction by Nebuchadnezzar and, ever since, a day of mourning for the Jews.

Josephus wrote in his history, perhaps at the command of Titus himself, that the destruction of the Temple was contrary to Titus' orders. Yet a fragmentary statement preserved by the 5th-century writer Sulpicius Severus throws a different light on this: "But others, including Titus himself, expressed the opinion that the temple ought to be razed in order that the Jewish and Christian religions might more completely be abolished; for . . . the Christians were an offshoot of the Jews, and if the root were taken away the stock would easily perish."

The Temple was never rebuilt. Its sacred objects, including the seven-branched golden lampstand and the table of holy bread (shewbread), were taken to Rome as plunder. All these were displayed in Titus' victory celebration and later depicted on his marble arch of triumph in Rome.

The coins minted to celebrate Rome's victory in A.D. 70 were inscribed, *Judea capta*, a premature statement in view of the fact that some of the Jews held out against Rome for three more years. The stronghold of Macherus on the eastern shore of the Dead Sea fell after a siege. Finally, in A.D. 73, the almost impregnable mountain-top fortress of Masada near the western shore of the Dead Sea was besieged by the Tenth Legion and its auxiliaries, numbering ten thousand men in all. Inside what had been Herod's palace and other cliff-top buildings, the desperate Jewish defenders and their families, comprising nearly a thousand persons, killed themselves rather than be captured by the Romans. The seven women and children who survived by hiding in a cistern told the heroic story of the last days of Masada.

Chapter 29 Simon Bar Kosiba's Rebellion
A.D. 132-135

After half a century in which there was no open defiance of Rome, a second disastrous rebellion of the Jews broke out. It was precipitated by the decision of the Emperor Hadrian to rebuild Jerusalem as a Roman city and to erect within the ruined Temple area a temple to Jupiter. The doomed uprising was led by a great giant of a man, Simon, son of Kosiba. The spiritual leader of the revolt was the great Rabbi Akiba. He hailed Simon as the messiah sent to restore the kingdom of Israel and made a pun on his name, calling him Bar Kochba, meaning "son of the star." This was probably a messianic reference to the oracle, "a star shall come forth out of Jacob" (Num 24.17). Because Jewish Christians could not accept Bar Kosiba as the Messiah, the insurgents punished them as traitors.

Bar Kosiba's initial success in driving the Romans from Jerusalem changed to defeat with the arrival in Palestine of eight legions and numerous auxiliary troops. The Romans, according to their historian Dion Cassius, captured fifty rebel fortresses and nearly a thousand villages. More than half a million Jews were slaughtered, among them the "Ten Martyrs" led by Rabbi Akiba. Bar Kosiba made his last stand near Jerusalem but died in the ruins of Bether.

All hope for Jewish independence now ended. Some of Bar Kosiba's soldiers fled to caves in the cliffs and canyons of the Judean desert where their bones were discovered in 1962 during a search for additional Dead Sea Scrolls.

After the uprising, so many Jewish captives were sold into slavery that the price of slaves declined throughout the empire. Hunger and disease as well as slaughter and slavery virtually stripped Judea of Jewish inhabitants. The Romans made Jerusalem a Roman colony with the name of *Aelia Capitolina,* and the surviving Jews were forbidden, under penalty of death, to enter the city except on one day in the year.

This day was the 9th of Ab, the anniversary of the Temple's destruction both in 587 B.C. by Nebuchadnezzar and in A.D. 70 by the Romans. On this day the Romans allowed the Jews to mourn at the Western Wall, the retaining wall built by Herod for the Temple platform and the only part of the wall that had survived the city's destruction. According to the Talmud, it survived because the poor had contributed to its building. Believing that the Divine Presence had not moved from this wall during the Temple's devastation, the Jews continued to pray and mourn at this place. The sound of these laments caused non-Jews to name it the "Wailing Wall." Except after the crusader massacre in 1099 and during the Jordanian occupation of Jerusalem from 1948 to 1967, Jewish prayers have always been offered at the Western Wall.

So strictly did the Romans enforce the edict against Jews in Jerusalem after A.D. 135 that the Christian church in the city was forced to reorganize and, for the first time in its history, replace its Jewish-born bishop for one of Gentile birth. Bar Kosiba's war severed the last remaining links between Judaism and Christianity, and the once-flourishing groups of Jewish Christians mentioned in the New Testament disappeared.

The Romans even erased the Jewish name from the region and called Judea, *Syria Palestina.* The Jews were now completely deprived of their state and until the 20th century they remained a people without a country, a people scattered among the nations of the world. As the author of the *Apocalypse of Baruch* wrote, "Zion has been taken from us and we have nothing now save the Mighty One and His Law."

Part Eight
The People of Israel and the Land of Palestine

Chapter 30 The Survival of Judaism

The disasters of A.D. 70 and 135 did not bring Jewish history to an end because Israel, the people of God, had not been annihilated. Moreover, Judaism and the Scriptures still survived. Though Judea was no longer inhabited by a preponderance of Jews, the great mass of the Jewish people flourished in the communities of the dispersion.

The preservation of the Jewish national religion during this period of overwhelming catastrophe was largely due to Rabbi Yohanan ben Zakkai, a celebrated scholar and leader of the Pharisees. During the siege of Jerusalem in A.D. 70, it was rumored that ben Zakkai, foreseeing the fall of the city, had had himself concealed in a coffin and carried outside Jerusalem's walls to Vespasian's headquarters. He successfully persuaded the Roman general to spare the small town of Jamnia (Jabneel or Jabneh), about thirty miles west of Jerusalem.

After Jerusalem fell to the Romans, ben Zakkai made Jamnia the chief center of the surviving Jewish community and the seat of Jewish learning and law. The great Sanhedrin moved there and the ceremonies and practices of Judaism were carefully preserved in the academy of Jamnia. There young men who were trained to read and understand the Scriptures began to interpret Judaism, not from the point of view of political power, but in terms of obedience to the written and Oral Law. The rabbinical council of scholars established at Jamnia became the chief authority in Palestine for settling questions of religious law. It was probably due to controversies with the Christians that it became necessary for the council to establish the canon of the Scriptures at this time.

Faced with the fact that the sacrifices of the Temple had ceased, the Sanhedrin declared that prayer accompanied by deeds of kindness and mercy was as effective for the atonement of sins as the former sacrifices. Synagogues now took the place of the destroyed Temple. There was much to keep Jewish hope alive. Instead of the sacrifices there were now the feasts, fasts, and festivals; study, kindly deeds, and prayer. Instead of priests and the old priestly families there were now teachers to educate the young and scribes to explain the first five books of the Bible, the Torah. In every synagogue throughout the Jewish community, the five Torah rolls were revered as God's teaching and law and the record of his divine guidance of his people during their history. Despite the prohibition against carrying anything on the Sabbath, orthodox Jews are permitted to carry the Torah, from the belief that it is not a burden because it carries Israel.

In the great centers of Jewish learning and scholarship at Jamnia, Tiberias, Babylon, and elsewhere, the Scriptures survived and were transmitted with extraordinary care. The Old Testament had been created out of the lives of the ancient Hebrews. Their descendants created their lives out of the Scriptures, deriving from them not only the strength to survive, but also the determination and courage to maintain their identity. Henceforth the Hebrew Scriptures became the "portable fatherland" of the Jews.

Chapter 31 The Jews Outlive Change and Persecution

By the 1st century B.C. the dispersion of the Jews prompted the Greek geographer and historian Strabo to write, "Hardly a city of the civilized world has failed to absorb them." Before the Temple was destroyed, Jews used to travel to Jerusalem for the great feasts and festivals. According to Acts 2.9-10, Jewish pilgrims from fifteen countries, beginning with Parthia and Media and extending west to Rome, were in Jerusalem for the Feast of Weeks, or Pentecost. It has been estimated that by the beginning of the Christian era there were perhaps three million Jews living, not only in Palestine and Transjordan, but dispersed in Syria, western Asia Minor, Cyprus, the Greek islands, Rome and south Italy, Tunisia, Cyrenaica, Egypt, Arabia, Mesopotamia, Persia, and Armenia. In these places the Jews lived their own distinctive life, which was marked by their faith in God and their efforts to obey his Law. It was to some of these scattered groups that Paul, himself a Jew of the dispersion, first brought the gospel message. Thus the Jewish communities paved the way for the rapid spread of Christianity.

Though the Jews lost all political control over Palestine after the Romans suppressed Bar Kosiba's rebellion in A.D. 135, and Jews were forbidden to live in Jerusalem, small groups of them resumed their community life outside the Holy City. There, partly protected by Rome's recognition of Judaism as a legal religion, they lived fairly peacefully throughout the Roman and Byzantine era.

During this period, scholars and rabbis collected and developed Jewish law and thought and compiled the

Talmud. This (from the Hebrew *talmudh,* meaning "instruction" or "learning") is a vast anthology containing not only the Oral Law, which was believed to have been delivered to Moses at Sinai at the same time as the written Law, but also all the tradition, interpretation, legend, knowledge, ritual, ceremony, commentary, and homiletic material that the rabbis thought worthy of preservation. The Palestinian Talmud of about A.D. 400 was superceded by the longer Babylonian Talmud compiled in Babylonia about A.D. 500-550. This attained an almost Scriptural status and was regarded by orthodox Jews as "the backbone of Judaism."

The most famous school of Jewish scholars engaged in preserving the traditional text of the Scriptures were the Masoretes, a name derived from the Hebrew *masorah,* meaning "tradition." They were active in many centers from the 6th to the 10th century A.D., standardizing the wording, amassing notes on such matters as the occurrence of words, and devising a system of signs to indicate vowels. This latter became necessary because ancient Hebrew was written solely in consonants. Five generations of the Ben Asher family of Tiberias, Palestine, ending with Moses Ben Asher and his son Aaron, finally completed work on the Masoretic text just after A.D. 900. Modern English versions of the Old Testament are based on this Masoretic text as transcribed in 1008 in the codex preserved in Leningrad.

With the spread of the great monotheistic faith of Islam beginning in the 7th century and the establishment of an immense Arab empire from the Atlantic Ocean on the west, across north Africa and the Middle East, to central Asia in the east, the Jews faced conquerors who claimed exclusive possession of the truth. Persecutions and massacres followed. The Moslems found, however, that it was to their advantage to use the good offices of co-operative Jewish leaders in maintaining order in the disciplined Jewish communities within their vast empire. Thus in

Babylonia, Asia Minor, Egypt, North Africa, and Spain, the Jews enjoyed centuries of relative peace. They farmed their own lands, and worked in towns as artisans and merchants while the religious, and even the civil, affairs of their communities were administered by Jewish officials.

The Jews of Europe, despite instances of compulsory baptism in Spain and Gaul in the 7th century, and unceasing denunciations by Church councils, began to live in open communities. For several centuries, kings, local counts, and archbishops granted charters guaranteeing their rights to the Jewish communities. Individual Jews flourished as farmers, craftsmen, doctors, and merchants.

With the beginning of the crusades in 1096, however, calamity struck. Called "Christ killers," Jews were persecuted, massacred, and driven from the mainstream of medieval society. Because they were not allowed to own land, they became an urban people confined to their ghettos and permitted to engage only in petty trading and moneylending. In 1290 the Jews were expelled from England and a little later from France. There were pogroms in Spain, from which they were expelled in 1492. In Venice in 1516 a ghetto was established where Shakespeare's Shylock of the *Merchant of Venice* must have lived.

The rise of capitalism improved the condition of European Jews and finally the American and French revolutions led to their political freedom. In England the Reform Bill of 1832 gave Jews the same rights as Catholics and Dissenters. From Russia, however, following the assassination of Czar Alexander II in 1881 by an organization of terrorists, a new wave of Jewish persecution moved westward as far as France. It set in motion the immigration of some two and a half million Jews to the United States where some Jews had been prominent since colonial times. They have made enormous contributions in many fields to American life. Today the United States contains the largest Jewish community in the world.

Chapter 32 **Upheavals in Palestine**

A.D. 135-1800

The comparative tranquility that Palestine enjoyed in the Roman era, and later in the Byzantine, lasted until Islam's holy war broke out in the 7th century. Until then Jerusalem was, of course, a completely non-Jewish city, but, in their own communities outside the holy city, the Jews survived, having given up all attempts to free themselves from Roman domination. For their part, the Romans acknowledged Judaism as a lawful religion.

Palestine's many pagan cities, linked by a growing network of Roman roads, grew in population as imperial wealth was lavished upon them. The Romans organized the province as a confederation of cities, each ruled by a curia, or council, and a governing committee, with the surrounding villages subject to city control. Everywhere the amenities of Roman city life were introduced: forums, colonnaded streets, theaters, baths, aqueducts, temples, and stadiums.

Christianity, even before it ceased to be a persecuted religion, became an increasingly powerful factor in the life of Palestine. Early in the 3rd century, Christian pilgrims arrived to worship at the holy places, and, about twenty years later, Origen, a pioneer in the textual study of the Bible, founded a school for Christian scholars at Caesarea. There he compiled his famous *Hexapla*, an immense scholarly work on which Origen and his assistants labored for twenty-eight years. It contained the current text of the Hebrew Scriptures, the same text written in Greek letters, and four different Greek translations, all carefully arranged in six parallel columns.

After A.D. 313, when the Emperor Constantine decreed that all religions were to be tolerated, and later, when he became a patron of Christianity, the persecution of Christians ceased. The status of Palestine now changed. Instead of being an unimportant, remote province, it became the Holy Land toward which Christian thoughts turned. The emperor's mother, Helena, made a pilgrimage to Palestine's holy sites and was credited with the discovery of the True Cross. Following Helena, increasing numbers of pilgrims went to the Holy Land to see where Christ had lived and to collect relics. Monasteries and churches were built near the principal holy sites, and hospices were established for the accommodation of Christian travelers. The emperor and his mother built basilicas and other buildings at three holy places: the Church of the Nativity in Bethlehem, the Eleona, or Church of the Olive Trees, on the Mount of Olives, and the sumptuously decorated group of buildings at the Holy Sepulcher in Jerusalem. This outstanding group was solemnly dedicated in 335 in the presence of three hundred bishops brought by the imperial authorities from the entire region.

Half a century later Jerome, one of the greatest scholars of the Latin church, made his pilgrimage to the Holy Land and finally settled in Bethlehem where he presided over a monastery. It was there that, with the help of a Jewish rabbi, he completed his translation of the Hebrew text of the Old Testament for his epoch-making Latin version of the Bible, later known as the Vulgate.

Byzantine control of Palestine lasted from the 5th to the 7th century, when Arab tribes, converted by the prophet Mohammed to the new faith of Islam and fired with zeal for a holy war, swept through Syria on a wave of conquest. In 638, Christian Jerusalem surrendered to the caliph Omar, Mohammed's friend and successor and the ruler who made Islam an imperial power.

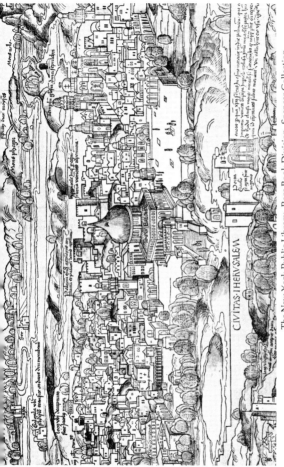

The City of Jerusalem—Erhard Reuwich (1486)

On his trip to the Holy Land in 1483, Reuwich sketched Jerusalem from the Mount of Olives, showing, in the background and to the right of the Dome of the Rock, the domed Church of the Holy Sepulcher with its double doorway. Woodcuts, based on Reuwich's drawings, illustrate Bernhard von Breydenbach's *Peregrinations*, printed in Mainz in 1486. Its fold-out map contains this detail and is the earliest printed illustration of genuine topographical importance.

The faith Mohammed introduced was the latest of the three monotheistic religions to originate in this region. According to its creed, there is no god but Allah and Mohammed is his prophet. Adam, Noah, Abraham, Moses, and Jesus are acknowledged as great prophets, for Mohammed had been influenced by Judaism and Christianity and had borrowed many elements from them. But he taught that he himself, as God's final and greatest prophet, offered mankind its highest form of religion. His vision of being transported to Jerusalem and ascending from the Holy Rock on Mount Moriah into heaven, where he received God's commandments, made that city the second most sacred Moslem place after Mecca. According to Moslem tradition, when the trumpet sounds on the Day of Judgment, God will judge all peoples from his throne on the Holy Rock.

This site, located on the Haram esh-Sherif, the walled platform on Mount Moriah, became the focus of Moslem piety after Omar established here a place of prayer. One of Omar's successors, the caliph Abd al-Malik, to surpass the splendor of the Church of the Holy Sepulcher, built, in 691, the Dome of the Rock, sometimes incorrectly referred to as the Mosque of Omar. It stands on the summit of Mount Moriah, on a massive rock outcropping that marks the site of Solomon's and Herod's former Temples and the location that figured in Mohammed's vision. Though the chief Moslem sanctuary was the Kaaba in Mecca, Abd al-Malik's purpose was to erect a rival sanctuary in Jerusalem. It is an octagonal structure crowned with a golden cupola and lavishly decorated inside and out in the Byzantine manner. Today, this earliest surviving monument of Islam, after many rebuildings, remains essentially the same as in the 7th century and is regarded as one of the most beautiful buildings in the world.

South of the Dome of the Rock and also on the Haram,

Abd al-Malik's son, al-Walid I, built the Mosque of el-Aqsa where its present highly-venerated successor now stands. Caliph al-Walid I, the greatest builder of the Omayyad dynasty, is notable as the earliest medieval ruler to erect hospitals for the sick, the blind, and the crippled.

Fortunately tolerance usually characterized Moslem policy toward Christians and Jews, because Jerusalem had now become a city holy to three faiths. Though the Jews no longer possessed a great sanctuary there, they built many synagogues in their own quarter of the city and were permitted to pray regularly at the Western Wall. The Moslems allowed Christian worship to continue; they also respected Christian churches and did not molest Christian pilgrims. Harun al-Rashid, the 8th-century caliph of Baghdad featured in the *Arabian Nights*, not only acknowledged the Emperor Charlemagne as protector of Jerusalem and owner of the Church of the Holy Sepulcher, but he established diplomatic relations with him. Charlemagne sent large sums of money to maintain and repair churches, monasteries, and hospices because the Christian community in the Holy Land was not self-supporting and depended on income from pilgrims and gifts from abroad. King Alfred of England, among other rulers, also sent gifts to Jerusalem.

Harassment of both Christians and Jews began after the Fatimid Dynasty of Egypt, a Moslem dynasty claiming descent from Mohammed's daughter, conquered Palestine in 969. In a period of increasing disorder, roving bands of Bedouin invaded the cities for plunder, or grazed their animals on carefully terraced and cultivated hillsides, thus breaking down retaining walls and causing the erosion that progressively ruined the land. When Al-Hakim, known as the Mad Caliph, declared himself divine, not only did he order forcible conversions to Islam, but in 1008 he also completely demolished the Church of the Holy Sepulcher. This outrage, added to the desecration of other Christian holy places, and the heavy taxes imposed on pilgrims by the barbarous Seljuk Turks, who had taken Jerusalem from the Fatimids in 1071, raised a clamor throughout Christendom for the rescue of the Holy Land from the infidels.

The First Crusade, organized by Pope Urban II, set out from Europe in 1096. In the Middle East, dissensions between the Seljuk Turks and the Fatimids resulted in the reconquest of Jerusalem by the Fatimids in 1098. The next year the crusaders, after furious onslaughts, captured the city. Because the leaders had lost control of their armies, horrible massacres ensued. Jerusalem now became the capital of the crusaders' Frankish Kingdom of Jerusalem, which was proclaimed on Christmas Day 1100.

The crusaders reconstructed many destroyed churches, adapted the Dome of the Rock for Christian worship, and rebuilt the Church of the Holy Sepulcher on the plan that largely survives today. An order of soldier-monks, the Knights Templars, became guardians of the temple area. They used the domed, octagonal shape of the Dome of the Rock, whose prototype had been the Church of the Holy Sepulcher, as a distinctive symbol on their armor, banners, and seals. They even reproduced its octagonal plan in churches and chapels of their order in England, such as the Temple Church in London and the Church of the Holy Sepulcher in Cambridge. In Palestine and Syria the Knights Templars and soldier-monks of other orders constructed a series of impressive Norman fortresses to defend the Holy Land against the Moslems.

Though unsuccessful crusades were launched almost continuously until the end of the 13th century, the Kingdom of Jerusalem ceased to be a functioning state after only eighty-eight years. In 1187 Saladin, in command of a zealous Moslem army, defeated the crusaders and re-established Moslem rule in the Holy Land. He pulled down the cross above the Dome of the Rock and cleansed the rock itself with rosewater to remove any remaining Christian taint from this Moslem shrine. With a generosity and chivalry that even his enemies acknowledged, he permitted Christian pilgrims to visit their shrines if they came unarmed. Jews were once again allowed to live in Jerusalem, as they have done ever since.

In 1453 the Ottoman Turks, having captured Constantinople, proceeded to establish a vast empire. They defeated the Mameluke rulers of Palestine near Aleppo in 1516, took Jerusalem, and for the next four hundred years ruled Palestine. The greatest of their sultans, Suleiman the Magnificent, a contemporary of the Emperor Charles V and King Henry VIII of England, ruled his huge empire during a time when Moslem literature, art, and architecture flowered. This period made its mark on Jerusalem. Suleiman ordered the city's disintegrating walls rebuilt, its gates restored, fountains constructed, and the Dome of the Rock adorned with exterior mosaics of glazed Persian tiles. Unfortunately the history of the long period of decline after Suleiman is little more than a chronicle of quarrels between the local sheiks, peasant oppression, and the general deterioration of the country.

Chapter 33 The Holy Land Today
1800-1980

Palestine experienced an awakening in the 19th century after Christian groups established monasteries and other religious communities there. Pilgrims, scholars, archaeologists, and tourists visited Jerusalem in increasing numbers. Roads were improved; the first railway was built by the French in 1880; foreign consulates and missions were opened to protect their own people. The Jewish inhabitants of Jerusalem increased from 1,500 in 1827 to 10,600 by 1873. Wealthy bankers of England and France helped the persecuted Jews of eastern Europe to emigrate to Palestine. There, after overcoming bitter hardships, they established flourishing agricultural settlements that inspired the dream of Zionism.

Zionism, the Jewish movement to transform barren Palestine into a fertile homeland for the Jews, gained momentum in the second half of the 19th century. In 1896, Theodor Herzl, a Viennese journalist, published his pamphlet, "The Jewish State," in which he proposed that Jewish workers, farmers, business men, and intellectuals unite to establish a Jewish homeland in Palestine. In the following year the first congress of the Zionist organization met in Switzerland.

During World War I, the British Foreign Secretary, Arthur Balfour, partly in recognition of the help given his government by the British chemist and Zionist, Chaim Weizmann, issued the Balfour Declaration of 1917. This declaration, which was endorsed by the principal Allied Powers, stated that the British government would use its "best endeavors" to help establish a national home for the Jews in Palestine, with the understanding that nothing would be done to prejudice the rights of non-Jews living there.

General Allenby, in command of British forces in Palestine during World War I, defeated the Turkish army opposing him and entered Jerusalem in December 1917. Despite the three-way struggle that ensued between the British, Jews, and Arabs, the area continued to be ruled by the British under a mandate of the League of Nations until 1948.

The General Assembly of the United Nations voted, on November 29, 1947, for the partition of Palestine into a Jewish and an Arab state. This move was largely based on two considerations: Many people thought that the Jews of Palestine were entitled to statehood because their community had increased to about half a million persons. Furthermore, it was urgently necessary to provide a home for the survivors of European Jewry who had recently escaped the Nazi holocaust in which six million Jews had perished.

On May 14, 1948, the day the British mandate ended, the independent State of Israel was proclaimed and a Jewish provisional government set up under the veteran statesman and politician, David Ben-Gurion. War against Israel had started in November when the United Nations passed its resolution for partition, but now it broke out in earnest between Israel and the Arab League. This was an association of Arab states, including Egypt, Jordan, Syria, Lebanon, Iraq, and Saudi Arabia, all of whom opposed the establishment of a Jewish state in what they regarded as the Arab land of Palestine. The Israeli War of Independence ended in 1949 with the defeat of the forces of the Arab League. The State of Israel was now in control of about eight thousand square miles, or approximately the area allocated to it in the United Nations resolution.

The first elections to the Israeli Parliament, the Knesset, were soon held and the provisional government was replaced by one that had parliamentary approval. The United States and the Soviet Union promptly recognized the new state, as did other nations, and in 1949 Israel was admitted to membership in the United Nations. At this time several hundred thousand Arabs left Israeli-controlled territory, while an equal number of Jews left Arab countries to settle in Israel. During the next four years, an influx of survivors from Hitler's extermination camps and settlers from communities in communist-dominated eastern Europe arrived in Israel. Thus the majority of Israel's population became Jewish.

With Israel's independence, peace did not come to this land whose boundary lines and sovereignty have so often been in dispute. Long before Abraham built his first altar at Shechem, this strategic area at the crossroads of ancient empires had been a place of raids, border clashes, fighting, massacres, and reprisals, as various groups struggled for power. All this continued in the 20th century as the Arabs fought to destroy the state of Israel and the Jews fought for their survival in three more wars: the Sinai War of 1956, the Six-Day War of 1967, and the Yom Kippur War of 1973. Though disengagements of forces and armistices were arranged, peace was not achieved because the religious, ethnic, political, and economic problems of the region continued to foster unrest, bitterness, and open hostility.

Despite unceasing threats to Israel's existence, its economy grew rapidly, aided by German reparations payments; United States aid; international loans; contributions, especially from Jews of the United States; as well as the intelligence, dedication, and hard work of the Israelis themselves. Since 1955 the total area of cultivable land has more than doubled, mostly due to irrigation. A pipeline was completed in 1964 to carry water from Lake Galilee to the Negev desert. The armistice line of the 1973 war enlarged Israel's territory to about thirty thousand square miles. Agriculture and industry have been promoted. By 1974, the population consisted of an estimated: 3,610,000 Jews; 392,500 Moslems; 84,500 Christians; 41,600 Druses and others.

In an unexpected and dramatic move, President Anwar el-Sadat of Egypt courageously flew to Jerusalem in November 1977 to confer with Prime Minister Menachem Begin and his cabinet and appear before the Knesset. This visit ended more than thirty years of confrontation and enmity between the two states and was the first step on the way to peace. Negotiations began and continued with many difficulties. Finally, at Camp David, the presidential retreat in the Maryland mountains, President Sadat and Prime Minister Begin, with the help of President Carter of the United States, agreed upon an outline for a peace treaty.

On a chilly day in early spring, March 26, 1979, the three leaders met again and, on the north lawn of the White House in Washington, D.C., in the presence of fifteen hundred invited guests and millions more watching television, signed the Arabic, Hebrew, and English versions of a formal peace treaty—the first between Israel and any Arab country. All three leaders spoke eloquent words of hope, despite the angry protests that were heard that day saying, "Down with Israel" and "Victory to Palestine." By coincidence the three leaders, Moslem, Jewish, and Christian, quoted the same prophecy spoken twenty-seven centuries ago in Jerusalem by one whom they all revere:

> And they shall beat their swords into plowshares,
> and their spears into pruning hooks;
> nation shall not lift up sword against nation,
> neither shall they learn war any more.
>
> Isaiah 2.4

President Carter, aware of the long road still ahead, closed his statement with the words, "So let us now lay aside war; let us now reward all the children of Abraham who hunger for a comprehensive peace in the Middle East. Let us now enjoy the adventure of becoming fully human, fully neighbors, even brothers and sisters."

Selected Bibliography

In addition to the books suggested for reading, study, or reference in the first two volumes of this series, *Introducing the Bible* and *A Guide to the Old Testament and the Apocrypha,* the following enrich our understanding of the history of Israel:

Aharoni, Yohanan and Avi-Yonah, Michael, *The Macmillan Bible Atlas.* New York: The Macmillan Company, 1968. Historical changes and events in Bible lands interpreted through a series of 262 maps, with a supplementary text.

Albright, William F., *The Biblical Period from Abraham to Ezra.* New York: Harper and Row, 1963. A short history of Old Testament times.

Avi-Yonah, Michael, ed., *A History of the Holy Land.* Translated by Charles Weiss and Pamela Fitton. London: Weidenfeld and Nicholson, Ltd., 1969. Palestine from prehistoric times to the present. Profusely illustrated.

Bright, John, *A History of Israel.* 3rd ed. Philadelphia: Westminster Press, 1972. A standard work.

de Vaux, Roland, *Ancient Israel: Its Life and Institutions.* Translated by John McHugh. New York: McGraw-Hill Book Co., Inc. 1961. By a renowned archaeologist and Biblical scholar.

Eban, Abba, *My People: The Story of the Jews.* New York: Random House, 1968. An eloquent history by an Israeli statesman. Illustrated.

Ehrlich, Ernst Ludwig, *A Concise History of Israel: From Earliest Times to the Destruction of the Temple in A.D. 70.* Translated by James Barr. New York: Harper and Row, Torchbooks, 1965. Readable and scholarly.

Grant, Michael, *Herod the Great.* New York: American Heritage Press, 1971. Well-documented and written. Illustrated.

Josephus Flavius, *The Jewish War.* Translated by G.A. Williamson. New York: Penguin Books, 1970. A contemporary account of the struggle against Rome.

Kenyon, Kathleen, *Archaeology in the Holy Land,* 3rd ed. New York: Praeger Publishers, 1970. By the Director of the British School of Archaeology in Jerusalem 1951-1963. Illustrated with drawings and photographs.

Pritchard, James B., ed., *The Ancient Near East: An Anthology of Texts and Pictures.* Princeton University Press, 1965. Basic material for a study of the Old Testament period.

Index